D0132540

"I HAD ONE OF THOSE"
TOYS
OF OUR GENERATION

"I HAD ONE OF THOSE"
TOYS
OF OUR GENERATION

ROBIN LANGLEY SOMMER

Crescent Books
New York/Avenel, New Jersey

Copyright © 1992 Brompton Books Corporation

All rights reserved. No part of this publication may be reproduced, stored in a retrieval system or transmitted in any form by any means, electronic, mechanical, photocopying or otherwise, without first obtaining written permission of the copyright owner.

This 1992 edition published by Crescent Books, distributed by Outlet Book Company, Inc., a Random House Company, 40 Engelhard Avenue Avenel, New Jersey 07001

Produced by Brompton Books Corporation 15 Sherwood Place, Greenwich, CT 06830

ISBN 0-517-06977-6

8 7 6 5 4 3 2 1

Printed and bound in Europe

To Eric and Ronnie and all the children

PAGE 1: **Rocking the cradle at a 1959 yo-yo contest.**

PREVIOUS PAGES: **(clockwise from top left) The Jetsons Fun Pad Game; Junior Erector set, from A. C. Gilbert; Mattel's Cheerful Tearful doll; Matchbox Models of Yesteryear; Hula Hoops, from Wham-O; and a selection of ever-popular Disney character figures.**

BOTTOM LEFT: **Chemcraft's "safe and exciting" atomic energy lab fascinates a budding nuclear scientist in 1948.**

BELOW: **A backyard fire chief saves the day.**

BOTTOM RIGHT: **Ready, set, go! The World Championship Toddlers Race, in Allentown, PA, gets underway at the height of the baby boom.**

CONTENTS

READY, SET, GO!

Never was a generation of children welcomed as warmly as that born after World War II. In our growing-up years, the 1950s and 1960s, we were listened to, catered to, and provided for in a way undreamed of by our parents' generation, which had struggled through Depression and world war. Like parents everywhere, American couples were determined that things would be better for their children. And they were. Future dads came back from overseas, and future moms happily traded wartime-industry jobs for snug houses in the suburbs where they could spend most of their time doting on us.

We had more playtime, more playthings, and more attention than any generation in history. And we took it quite happily for granted, as our birthright. We were the promise of a future free of conflict and want, moving steadily towards limitless prosperity and security. It was fun being a baby boomer, and we took full advantage of it. Nothing was too good for us. We had plenty of playmates, too. Some 76,500,000 babies were born in America between 1946 and 1964.

The purpose of this book is to look back with laughter at all those toys we lived with and loved when the world was a simpler place. So strap on your cap guns and saddle up. In the immortal words of the Lone Ranger, "Hi-yo, Silver! Away!"

LEFT: **A world of your own (where YOU were the boss) came with that long-awaited Lionel train set.**

RIGHT: **The good life in 1955: A handsome young family, a modest dream house, and a Chevy convertible with whitewall tires.**

The toy fads of the postwar years had one thing in common – action. Slinky spring toys bounded down the stairs end over end. FRISBEES whizzed across back yards, and Wham-O Super Balls ("four times more bouncy, four times more fun!") sprang to new heights. One hundred million Hula Hoops twirled around a like number of kids. Whizzler tops took off humming and worked up to a high-pitched shriek guaranteed to send your parents screaming into the night. Silly Putty was applied indiscriminately to walls, carpets, and pets by enthusiastic young creators. Yo-yos in dazzling fluorescent colors flashed up and down all over the country. We were an active generation, and, when one fad played itself out, we were quick to embrace another. Meanwhile, an army of child psychologists, pediatricians, and social scientists assured our fatigued parents that all this activity was *good* for us. They were on our side.

Surprisingly, a lot of the ideas and technology for the new and updated toys came out of the austere war years. Intensive research and development into alternate sources of scarce commodities like rubber and tin resulted in new products that soon made their way to the toy shelves. Wham-O's Super Ball, made of a high-resilience compound called Zectron, spawned a lot of competitive products with less bounce to the ounce. Finally, Wham-O's copywriters tried to flatten competitors by announcing "the granting of United States Patent #3,241,834 covering the chemical composition of . . . Super Balls, the products that changed an industry." The kids didn't pay much attention – as usual.

Slinky was the brainchild of a wartime naval engineer inspecting a ship in a Philadelphia dockyard. When Richard James saw a torsion spring fall off a table and bounce around, he was intrigued and took it home with him. After experimenting with different types of steel for several years, Mr. James and his wife, Betty James, introduced the coiled spring as a toy named Slinky in Philadelphia's Gimbel's department store. At rest, Slinky wasn't too prepossessing, but after watching it walk down a slanted board at the demonstration counter, some 400 people walked out with 400 Slinkys at a dollar apiece. James Industries was off to a flourishing start.

Forty-six years later, the company is still producing Slinky and its variations, including a smaller-size spring and one made of plastic. It has also been sold as an expandable pull toy with animal heads and tails or train parts attached to either end, but the basic design has never changed. In all its various incarnations, Slinky has been a hit with kids right down to the present day.

Another postwar fad that came to stay is Silly Putty, invented by James Wright during his wartime work as a chemical engineer for General Electric. The pinkish silicone compound was intended to be a synthetic rubber substitute and it did, in fact, bounce and stretch like the natural product, but it snapped when it was stretched too far. Wright thought the compound had potential as a plaything. He called it Gooey Gupp and sold it at a toy store in New Haven, Connecticut, until 1949. Then an entrepreneur named Peter Hodgson bought the rights and repackaged the product as Silly Putty, advertised as "the real solid liquid." It is manufactured by Binney & Smith, a company formed in 1900 to make carbon black and slate pencils. The firm now offers Silly Putty in plastic-egg packages of yellow, green, and blue, in addition to the original red, in which 32 million chunks of the stretchy stuff were sold within five years.

Silly Putty was one of the first children's products to capitalize on the new medium of television in both advertising and packaging (the egg's cardboard container was shaped like a TV screen). One of the best things about it was that you could use it to pick up images from comic books, newspapers, and other reading matter.

MOST FANTASTIC BALL EVER CREATED BY SCIENCE!

AM-O

SUPER·BALL

50,000 LBS. OF COMPRESSED ENERGY

AMAZING FUN!

made of NEW AMAZING ZECTRON

FOR ALL BALL GAMES

BASEBALL
PINNERS
JACKS
ETC.

IT'S ALMOST ALIVE!

Introducing "SLINKY"

1947 TOY FAIR

JAMES INDUSTRIES
TORONTO ONTARIO

DISTRIBUTED BY

IN THE EAST   IN TH
BONDED PRODUCTS MFG. CO.   MACKEL
MONTREAL   WIN

THE ORIGINAL Spring TOY
Slinky

THE ORIGINAL SPRING TOY
Slinky

U.S. PATENT NO.

FUN FOR YOUNG AND OLD

PREVIOUS PAGES: **Wham-O executives at a top-secret board meeting to discuss new-product ideas.**

LEFT: **Wham-O ad copy soars to Super Ball heights.**

ABOVE: **The energetic Slinky would have looked at home in a hardware store.**

ABOVE: **Slinky does its stuff at the 1947 Toy Fair.**

LEFT: **Betty James and associates at James Industries in Hollidaysburg, Pennsylvania, with their brainchild.**

TOP RIGHT: **A cartoon ad for Silly Putty's 40th anniversary in 1990.**

ABOVE: **The famous Silly Putty egg-shaped container and TV-screen-shaped packaging.**

11

Connecticut Yankee tinsmiths and traders had been famous for their toys since colonial days, so it's not surprising that the FRISBEE got its start on the New Haven campus of Yale University. There, undergraduates of the Jazz Age amused themselves by throwing around pie tins from the nearby Frisbie Baking Company. Unwitting pedestrians were warned of a flying tin by the cry "Frisbie!" – comparable to "Fore!"

The pastime really got off the ground in 1948, when a Californian named Fred Morrison used a new flexible plastic to design a disc whose flight could be controlled by wrist action. He sold the idea to the energetic Wham-O people, who brought it to market as the Pluto Platter, with an eye to the prevailing interest in UFOs and outer space. However, the Walt Disney Company's popular cartoon dog, Pluto, led to confusion about the name, so it was changed to FRISBEE. As such, it's been flying high ever since, in a rainbow of colors and even a glow-in-the-dark model – some hundred million sold to date. The 1980s brought the sophisticated Whoosh and Aerobie versions, but it's still your basic flying saucer. FRISBEE!

Wham-O brought out another winner in 1958, when it introduced the Hula Hoop to American kids. Founders Arthur Melin and Richard Knerr, whose first product was the famous Slingshot that gave Wham-O its name, had seen Australian kids using a bamboo hoop for exercise while on a trip Down Under. Initially, they made the toy of wood and demonstrated it in California schoolyards. When it caught on, Wham-O moved to plastic hoops for mass production. Twirling the brightly colored hoops became a national craze, especially after one was featured on the popular "Dinah Shore Chevy Show." The Hula Hoop marathon was on, and within a year, it had circled the globe. Torsos were twirling all over Europe, Japan, South Africa . . . and a group of Belgian explorers even took the fad to the South Pole. Wham-O's competitors came out with a bunch of "me too" hoops until the middle 1960s, when the craze died out, but Wham-O has since copyrighted both the name Hula Hoop and the idea. At this writing, Hula Hoops are still with us, the only difference being that they have little plastic pellets inside that make a "shoop shoop" sound as they go round and round.

TOP LEFT: **The original "Pluto Platter" with its prototype, the Frisbie pie tin.**

ABOVE: **A FRISBEE-throwing contest for 100 participants — serious business!**

LEFT: **Height makes right in a pick-up FRISBEE game on the campus of North Carolina State University.**

RIGHT: **Hula Hoop silliness at its peak in a 1958 marathon without a lunch break.**

LEFT: A Hula Hoopster takes to the sky from a trampoline, while another skillfully spins five hoops simultaneously. What a gas!

RIGHT: Making like a circus seal with the versatile Wizzzer top.

FAR RIGHT: The Gyroscope was another popular takeoff on the top. Here, a young expert gives a "gyrosnoot" demo – the nose knows.

BELOW: The Hula Hoop craze took off twirling in – you guessed it – California.

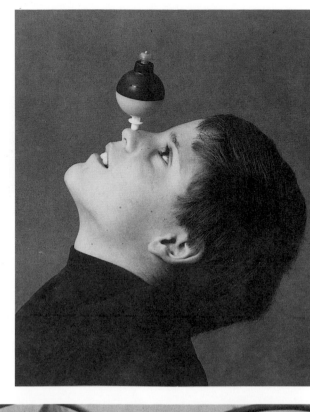

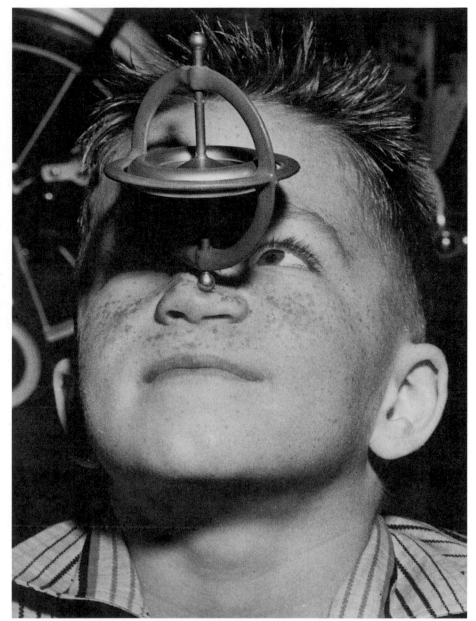

That venerable toy the top evolved from its humble origins on the floor into an acrobatic noisemaker when Amsco brought out its Whizzler in the late 1950s. The Whizzler was suspended in the middle of a nylon cord and started humming when you pulled on the cord. Soon it was spinning faster and faster and emitting a piercing screech that went on and on. For 79 cents, you could alarm the entire block. But sooner or later, someone would shriek "Stop that!" and the Whizzler would have to be retired.

Another acrobatic top (noiseless, unfortunately) was the MagneTop, which could balance on a wire as it spun, thanks to its built-in magnet. The Whee-Lo also did a spinning wire-walk act. The Matchbox Company's Wizzzer ("the world's wildest whirler!") was a floor-based toy with a friction motor activated by its rubber tip. It spun at a dizzying rate ("over 10,000 rpm!!") until the motor ran down. Matchbox is still turning out Wizzzers, along with the miniature cars for which it is famous. Kenner's Screecher Siren was set off by a plastic Spin Stick. This 1971 innovation not only screeched at a hair-raising decibel rate, but it also threw off sparks and launched a flying saucer!

LEFT: The "rock the cradle" trick went fine, and so did the "double delight," but overconfidence finally unstrung this contestant.

RIGHT: It was hard to misplace a brightly colored Cheerio yo-yo.

BELOW: The right model could take you all the way to the Yo-Yolympics, sponsored by Duncan.

Toymakers Louis and Dave Marx had revived another centuries-old toy – the yo-yo – in the late 1920s, when they sold millions of wooden models. Donald Duncan got into the yo-yo game in 1929 with great success, but the fad died out after the Depression. Twenty years later, Duncan contracted with the Flambeau Corporation to make yo-yos of brightly colored plastic instead of wood. Kids scooped up the flashy new models at the rate of 16 million a year during the 1960s. Yo-yo tricks and contests abounded, and the toy became so popular that it went full circle – back to specially handmade wooden models for yo-yo "pros." In 1969 Flambeau became Duncan's parent company, and the future of the yo-yo is still looking bright.

Uneeda had been making dolls since World War I, but it sprang into prominence during the 1960s with its bizarre miniature Troll dolls, topped by wiggy-looking "hair" in psychedelic colors. So captivating were these gargoylish little creatures that they soon increased in size from four inches to a foot, sporting bushy topknots ranging from bright green to fluorescent orange. They were ugly, but kids loved them. Trolls made a comeback in the 1980s, when a new generation discovered them.

One toy that parents loved on sight was Parker Brothers' Nerf ball, a soft, sponge-rubber item that came out in the late 1960s. You could play with it in the house, because it was nearly weightless and thus harmless to lamps, vases, and other cherished household items. Nerf soon appeared with a whole line of popular accessories, from basketball hoops to flyweight baseball bats. Parental nerves relaxed under the

ABOVE: **Clackers – a pair of plastic balls you could swing and bounce off each other – had an enthusiastic following, until the FDA issued a warning in 1971 that the plastic sometimes shattered.**

RIGHT: **Parker Brothers' package directions for Instant Insanity advised the puzzle-solver to "be calm." It wasn't easy to stay calm, and it was close to impossible to do the puzzle.**

TOP RIGHT: **Supersoft Nerf balls for indoor play were the answer to a parent's prayer.**

sound of (near) silence. Not least because parents love them nearly as much as kids do, Nerf products have made their way into the 1990s.

Parker Brothers struck gold again with Instant Insanity, a plastic puzzle composed of four cubes with different-colored sides. The trick was to stack the cubes so that each side of the stack showed four different colors – maddening! This aptly named game sold 7 million copies in 1968 and was followed closely by Parker Brothers' Soma – another deceptively simple-looking puzzle in which you tried to assemble a cube from seven pieces. Later, an even more torturous refinement of these games was introduced as the Rubik's Cube.

While newfangled toys came and went, some games never went out of fashion. Children's fascination with the smooth colorful balls known as marbles has endured since ancient times. Marbles were still a popular toy in nineteenth-century England, where schoolboys shot against each other in circles drawn on the ground. During the American Civil War, a militant toymaker named Joel Ellis came up with a toy cannon that could shoot a marble almost 60 feet. At that time, marbles were imported from Europe, but in the 1880s, American companies began to make them in clay. One of the first was the Samuel C. Dyke Company of South Akron, Ohio, which turned out some 30,000 marbles a day in the 1890s.

Then other Ohio firms began to produce the glass marbles that became a staple of back yard and schoolyard play – rainbows, aggies, moonies, cat's eyes, jumbo shooters. The kid who could shoot the straightest went home with the marbles.

LEFT: **A boy's best friend intently follows the progress of a marble game.**

RIGHT: **Ideal's Kerplunk was accurately described as "a tantalizing game of nerve and skill."**

BELOW: **Many a Saturday afternoon was spent dueling for possession of a friend's most colorful (and coveted) marble.**

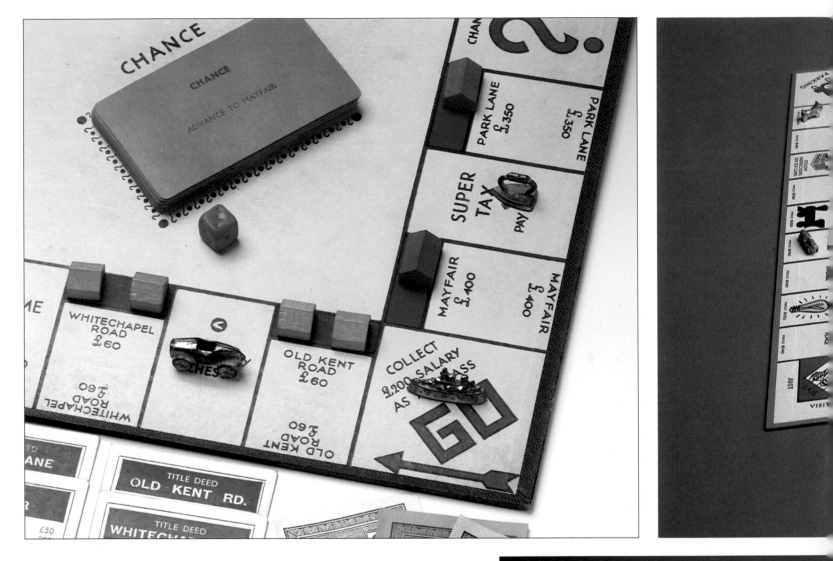

In the 1920s, Berry Pink Industries of New York began to market them through its subsidiary, Marble King. During the 1950s and 1960s, these time-honored playthings became a craze. Trouser knees were worn through as would-be marble kings staked everything on a straight shot at their opponent's favorite.

Amsco came out with a spiral plastic toy called the Marble Raceway, which got the game off the ground and turned it into a contest of speed rather than skill. First marble to the bottom of the spiral was the winner. And there were several variations on the marble labyrinth theme, in which you pushed and pulled levers to send your marble through an obstacle course. In the game called Kerplunk, you poured marbles into the top of a clear plastic cylinder. Midway down the cylinder you had stuck in a number of plastic picks. The trick was to pull out the picks without triggering the marbles to crash to the bottom.

Board games came into their own when we were growing up. They proliferated in every Christmas catalog and were published for every age group, interest group, and level of complexity. The best seller of all was, and still is, Parker Brothers' Monopoly, which came out in 1935. Kids got a chance to practice some real-life skills like banking, real estate transactions, and dealing with the unexpected – "Go directly to Jail. DO NOT PASS GO, DO NOT COLLECT $200." Grown-ups loved Monopoly too, and a rainy-day game could turn into a weekend marathon. Parker

Brothers estimates that more than 250 million people have played the game, which is licensed in over 30 countries.

Each Monopoly set comes complete with playing pieces, $15,000-plus in play money, two sets of cards from which to draw at the roll of the dice, and an assortment of little plastic (formerly wooden) houses and hotels to put on your properties as you go around the board. The street names for the properties come from Atlantic City, New Jersey – hence Boardwalk, which becomes Mayfair in the U.K., where Park Place is called Park Lane. Charles Darrow, who designed the game, misspelled the name of Atlantic City's Marven Gardens, and it still appears as "Marvin" Gardens on the Monopoly board.

At first, Parker Brothers rejected Darrow's idea for Monopoly, but the company thought better of it when Darrow began to sell the game himself in 1934. A year later, everyone concerned was getting rich, in the true Monopoly spirit. Darrow became a world traveler and collector of rare orchids, while Parker Brothers got out from under the Great Depression well ahead of most American businesses.

Monopoly was a logical extension of the company's first game, Banking, which had been invented by 16-year-old George S. Parker in 1883. Five years later, his brother Charles joined him in the business. Parker Brothers would publish more than 1200 games before being acquired by General Mills in the late 1960s. Now it is part of Kenner Products.

ABOVE: **The winner and still champion: Parker Brothers' Monopoly, the best-selling board game of all time.**

TOP LEFT: **Pound notes and London streets identify the U.K. edition of Monopoly, by Waddington Games Ltd.**

FAR LEFT: **A variety of challenging games from Parker Brothers, which was acquired by Kenner Products almost 100 years after 16-year-old George S. Parker founded the company in 1883.**

ABOVE: **Clue, the U.S. version of Waddington's Cluedo, lets everyone become a detective to solve an Agatha Christie-style murder in a country house.**

LEFT AND BELOW: **Milton Bradley's Chutes & Ladders and Candy Land put little kids into the board-game picture, too.**

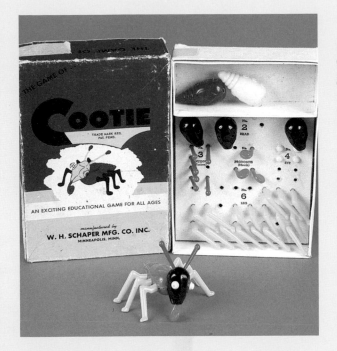

Parker Brothers brought many successful games to market during the 1950s and 1960s. They included Clue (by arrangement with Waddington Games Ltd. of Leeds, England), Career (advertised "for ages 8 to 80"), Sorry, Risk, Dig, and Mille Bornes, or "A Thousand Milestones" – a fast-moving travel game from France. But the company's fastest mover is still Monopoly, with some 100 million sets sold to date. Its players have set records of every conceivable (and wacky) kind, from longest game between two players (80 hours) to smallest game board (1 inch). Monopoly has been played in elevators, fire trucks, underground, upside down, on balance beams, and underwater.

College students have excelled in setting such records as the largest Monopoly game ever. It was played at Juniata College in Huntingdon, Pennsylvania, in 1967. There the playing board was more than a block square, with campus streets and sidewalks standing in for the familiar properties. Big foam-rubber dice were thrown from a third-floor fire escape, and players were kept in touch by bicycle and walkie-talkie. At the University of Pennsylvania, haggard players ran out of Monopoly money after 160 hours and wired an SOS to Parker Brothers. A million dollars worth of play money was dispatched via Brink's armored car, complete with armed guard, and the game went on.

Milton Bradley was the other master of the board game. Aside from such perennial favorites as Chutes and Ladders (Snakes and Ladders in the U.K.), Candy Land, Go to the Head of the Class, and Easy Money, MB was responsible for The Game of Life, an updated version of a game the company first marketed in the mid-nineteenth century. This was the prototypical gimmick board game of the baby boom years. With a plastic spinner instead of dice or cards, and little plastic cars to move around the board, The Game of Life rewarded players for filling their cars with plastic blue and pink pegs representing children. Henceforth cardboard playing surfaces would be festooned with plastic formations, or dispensed with entirely in favor of colorful plastic three-dimensional objects that were an integral part of the game itself.

ABOVE: **Schaper's build-a-bug Cootie game invariably sent players into gales of laughter.**

BELOW: **Linking up those chimps in Lakeside's Barrel of Monkeys was harder than it looked.**

BELOW RIGHT: **Milton Bradley's Game of Life was the first three-dimensional board game, with integral plastic structures and an elaborate plastic spinner.**

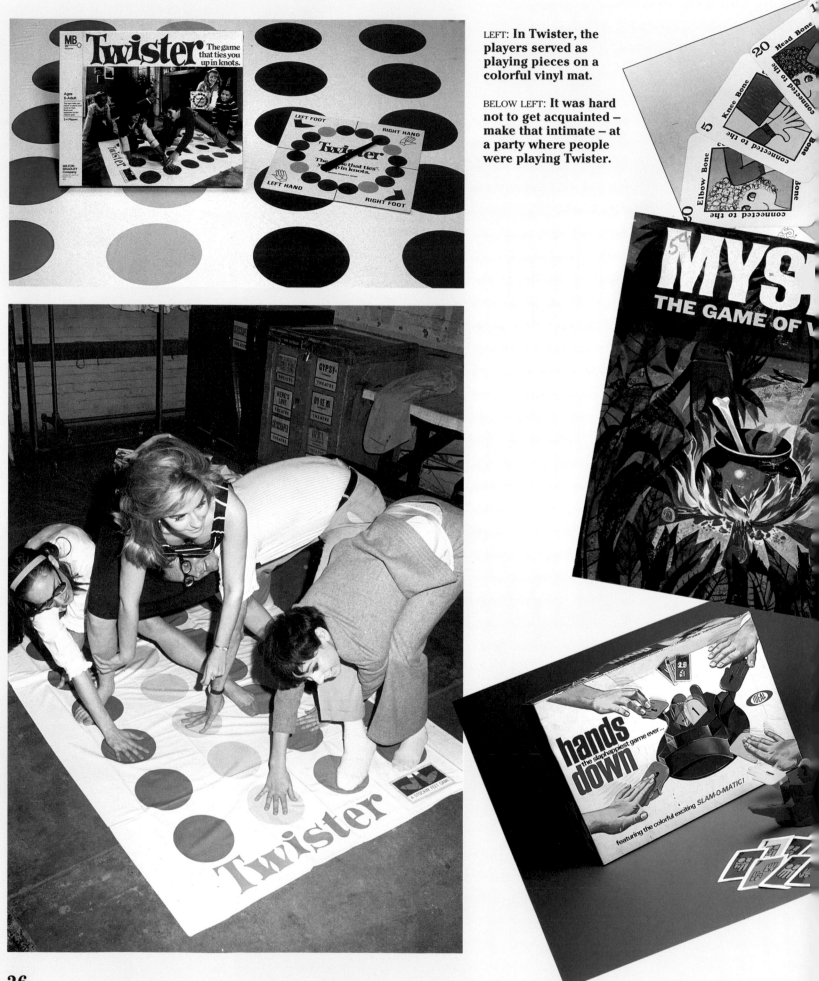

LEFT: In Twister, the players served as playing pieces on a colorful vinyl mat.

BELOW LEFT: It was hard not to get acquainted – make that intimate – at a party where people were playing Twister.

In Mouse Trap, a 1963 offering from Ideal, players constructed an elaborate three-dimensional trap by pressing plastic pieces onto the playing board. The completed trap didn't always work, but that was part of the fun. Over a million games were sold in the first year. In the game called Cootie (kidspeak for "louse"), you put a plastic bug together as directed by rolls of the dice. From this modest beginning, woodworker Herb Schaper turned his hobby of whittling fishing lures into the Schaper line of 40 toys and games.

Lakeside's Barrel of Monkeys challenged you to pick up 12 plastic chimps in a row by their hook-shaped arms. Usually the chain would break and the chimps would fall, and you had to start over. The monkeys were bigger in the Giant Barrel of Monkeys and easier to hook together, but if you were little it got pretty tricky when the chain got so long that you had to hold it up high over your head and stand on your toes to get those last monkeys.

Hot Potato was an energetic game in which players tossed around a plastic potato with a wind-up timer. The loser was left holding the potato when the timer went off. The same principle applied in Milton Bradley's Time Bomb game, in which a plastic bomb equipped with a wind-up fuse went off with an unnerving bang when time ran out. They were great party games.

Another great party game, and one of the most enduring fads of the 1960s, was Milton Bradley's Twister, a hilarious match between people and plastic. Twister's "game board" was a big vinyl floor mat imprinted with circles of different colors. Moves were dictated by spinning an arrow to color-coded directions about where to place one's hands and feet ("right foot on yellow," "left hand on blue," etc.). Soon players were contorted all over the mat, and if more than two people got involved, all bets were off.

Twister was introduced in 1966, and demonstrated on "The Tonight Show" – with uncontrollable mirth – by Johnny Carson and Eva Gabor. The craze was on, and Milton Bradley was the uncrowned king of the game fads. Competitors soon rushed to market with comparable "live" board games such as Funny Bones, from Parker Brothers. Here the moves were directed by game cards that told you, for example, to connect your head bone to your partner's elbow bone, or you knee bone to his hand bone.

Gimmickry got supernatural in the early 1950s with games like Ideal's Magic "8 Ball," which is still on the market. You read your fortune through a little window in the base of a plastic "billiard ball." The ball is filled with liquid that contains a many-sided piece imprinted with various fortunes. Players ask the magic ball a question, then turn it over to find their fate.

Another otherworldly item was the "mysterious moving skull" that came with Ideal's Mystic Skull board game. Losers in this voodooish contest could end up in a tiny cooking pot designed for "human sacrifices." Less bloodcurdling, but still uncanny, were the Amazing Kreskin ESP Game, the Green Ghost Game (in which the ghost glowed in the dark), and the Mystery Zodiac Game, all of which haunted the late 1960s.

Milton Bradley's Mystery Date was directed at young girls, who played the fantasy board game to find out whether their date behind the plastic door would be a "dream" or a "dud." As in real life, the duds far out-

TOP: **Funny Bones was another game that used players as live game pieces to hilarious efffect.**

ABOVE: **Board games got eerie with Ideal's Mystic Skull, "The Game of Voodoo."**

LEFT: **Ideal's Hands Down was, as advertised, slaphappy.**

numbered the dreams. Boys gravitated toward Marx's Rock 'Em Sock 'Em Robots. This pugnacious game featured a red and a blue robot slugging it out in a ring, operated by hand controls at ringside. The contenders kept swinging until a poke in the jaw made the loser's head pop up.

Ideal had another hit with Hands Down, a fast-moving game played with a plastic centerpiece dubbed "Slam-O-Matic." Up to four players drew numbered cards and tried to be first to slap their hands onto the hand-shaped plastic molds.

Kohner Brothers revved up basic roll-the-dice board games with its "Pop-O-Matic" feature, centered in games like Trouble and Headache. The dice were contained in a clear plastic dome that players pushed down and let go. A hidden spring popped the dome back up and scrambled the dice for the next move. Another popular Kohner toy was Hats Off, in which players catapulted plastic hats into designated slots on the game board.

Milton Bradley's Operation gave aspiring surgeons a chance to practice on a cardboard patient. The object was to remove various "body parts," including a funny bone, with a pair of tweezers connected to a buzzer. If you didn't perform the operation deftly enough, the buzzer shrilled and the patient's nose lit up in an alarming way. Kids who were really phobic about doctors and hospitals didn't do very well at this game, which is still on the market.

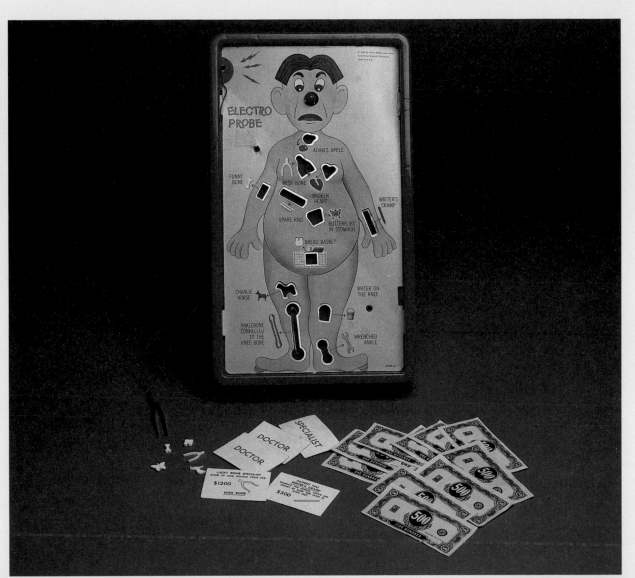

ABOVE: **Selchow & Righter's Scrabble was a godsend to word buffs – far better than a crossword puzzle.**

RIGHT: **Operation was not a game for the faint-hearted.**

LEFT: **Milton Bradley's Battleship was a popular war game targeted at boys and their dads.**

RIGHT: **Yahtzee, combining chance and skill, was the thinking kid's game.**

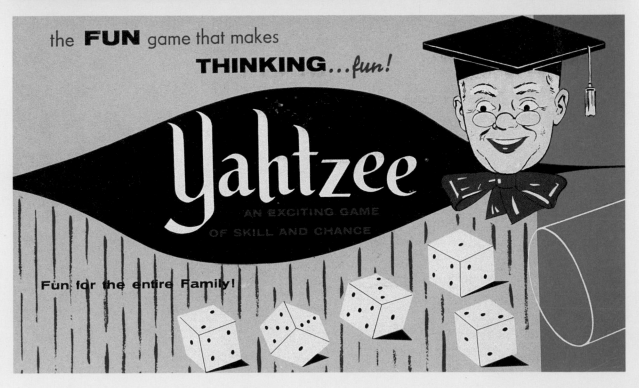

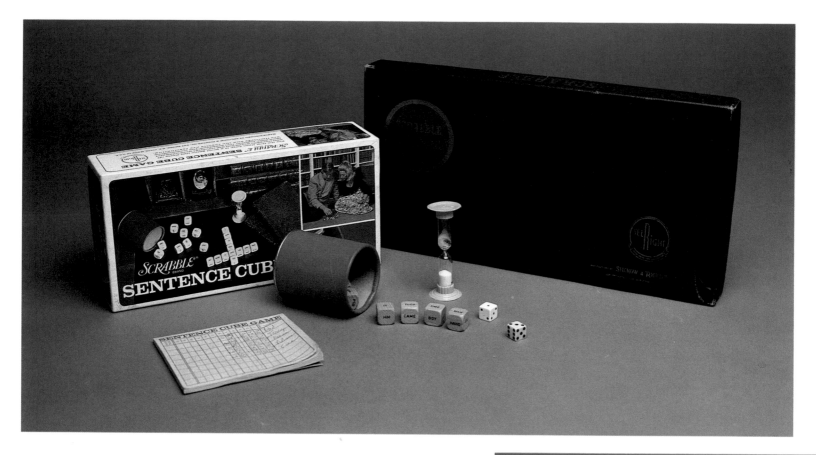

The Vietnam War decreased the demand for war toys, but, oddly enough, war games remained popular in the late 1960s. Milton Bradley's Stratego, designed for older players, was a board game of battle strategy. Battleship kept you guessing about the location of enemy ships so that you could blow them up before they got you.

Another game geared to the more sophisticated player was Yahtzee, which was introduced by Edwin S. Lowe in the early 1950s. A board game that combined the elements of dice and poker, it was advertised as "the fun game that makes thinking . . . fun!" and there was a little professor on the package. Lowe's career had been launched by bingo games in the 1920s, and he capitalized on his success with Yahtzee with such games as Scribbage, Real Bingo, Chess Tutor, and Bet-A-Million.

A long-time gamemaker, Selchow and Righter (the creators of Parcheesi in 1867), surpassed its expectations with Scrabble. The intriguing word game caught on instantly and is now available in seven languages. Its wooden tiles can be combined into more than three billion seven-letter configurations. Scrabble is still selling at the rate of two million sets per year, to the joy of word buffs everywhere. Ongoing Scrabble clubs meet and play tournaments all over the country, adding a social dimension to the game's test of language skills.

The television age speeded up the trend towards all kinds of sport games that had started in the mid-1930s. At that time, a new firm called Cadaco-Ellis (now Cadaco) produced a game called Varsity Football, whose success inspired the introduction of Bas-Ket, Pro Foto-Football, and All-Star Baseball.

Bas-Ket used a small celluloid basketball on a three-dimensional court. Levers shot the ball at the basket from a dozen holes spaced around the court. During the 1960s, Rapid Mounting and Finishing

TOP LEFT: **The Scrabble Sentence Cube game was a refinement aimed at true Scrabble aficionados.**

ABOVE: **Parker Brothers' Pit taught you how to trade commodities futures, while Boggle baffled even the keenest wordmakers.**

LEFT: **The Today game played off the popularity of the morning TV show hosted by Dave Garroway.**

RIGHT: **Cadaco's All-Star Hockey game put its players right into the action.**

bought Cadaco and reissued its original Varsity Football game as All-American Football.

In time, game layouts became more detailed and there were tie-ins to popular athletes and teams. Bas-Ket became NBA Bas-Ket and a Match Point Tennis game and All-Star Hockey game were added to the line. Cadaco also sold a portable Fun 'n' Games Table Set with some 15 game boards on it. The table and two stools folded up for easy transport. The economy was booming, and Americans were – as always – on the go.

The first electric sports game had come out in the 1940s, when the Electric Game Company of Holyoke, Massachusetts, offered its Electric Baseball, Football, and Bowling games. Plastic players faced off on a metal surface that moved them around as it vibrated. A screw at the end of the game field controlled the degree of vibration, moving the players at a pace from slow motion to top speed.

The Gotham Pressed Steel Corporation introduced some refinements that made the original games more exciting and true to life. Its early 1960s electric football game included a grandstand, bleachers, and tiny NFL pennants. But it was still pretty noisy, like most of the electric games. And if you turned the power up too high, electric game figures tended to shoot off in all directions. Or they all fell down.

Innovative Tudor Metal Products Corporation had several entries in the electric game sweepstakes, including Horse Race, with jockies, and Harness Race, with sulkies, on circular tracks. Tudor also made a game called Track Meet; its deluxe version, Track and Field Meet, included discus, javelin, and pole vault features.

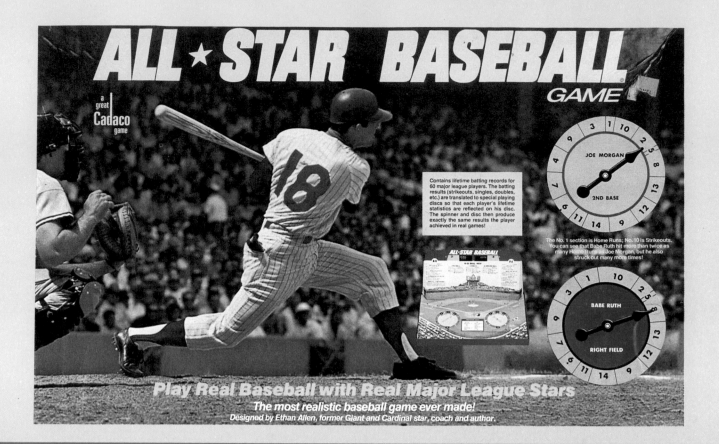

Contains lifetime batting records for 60 major league players. The batting results (strikeouts, singles, doubles, etc.) are translated to special playing discs so that each player's lifetime statistics are reflected on his disc. The spinner and disc then produce exactly the same results the player achieved in real games!

The No. 1 section is Home Runs; No. 10 is Strikeouts. You can see that Babe Ruth hit more than twice as many Home Runs as Joe Morgan, but he also struck out many more times!

Play Real Baseball with Real Major League Stars

The most realistic baseball game ever made!
Designed by Ethan Allen, former Giant and Cardinal star, coach and author.

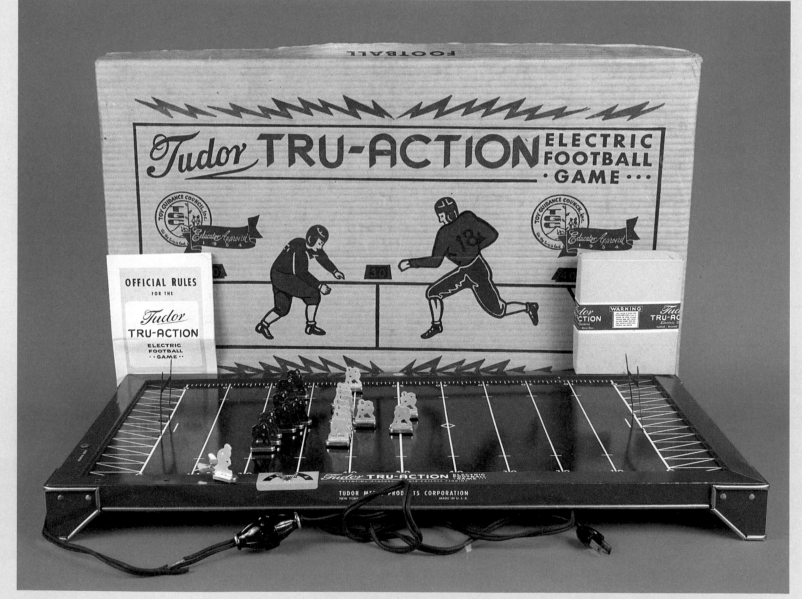

LEFT: **Cadaco's All-Star Baseball game had a 3-D ballpark and playing discs imprinted with major players and their statistics.**

BOTTOM LEFT: **An early entry into the electric sports-game field – Tudor's Tru-Action Football set.**

BELOW: **NBA Bas-Ket delivered on its promise of "Fast Action Sports Fun!"**

BELOW RIGHT: **A late 1960s advertisement for Aurora's popular Skittle-Bowl, based on a classic game from the U.K.**

BOTTOM: **Atari's Pong: the video game that started a new craze in 1974.**

Hockey games were popular in both electric and mechanical models. Gotham made a mechanical Pass 'n' Shoot Basketball game, in which players could also defend against shots. And Hubley's mechanical Golferino, a nine-hole tabletop miniature course, had a big following.

Merdel Manufacturing branched off from long-established Carrom Industries during the 1960s to concentrate entirely on toys. (Later they bought the familiar Carrom name.) Their best-known product was the versatile Carrom set, a reversible wooden game board with corner pockets and many different playing pieces. You could use it to play chess, checkers, crokinole, backgammon, pocket billiards – up to 100 different games. Other popular Carrom games included Skittles, Kikit, and Nok-Hockey.

Pong, the father of all electronic games, looks primitive now, but it was mesmerizing in 1974, when the Atari Corporation brought it to home TV screens. The "ping-pong net" split the screen down the middle, and the blip that acted as the ball bounced off the sides of the screen at odd angles. Players controlled the electronic paddles with tabletop knobs, and the volleys got faster the longer you kept them going. It was addictive. With Pong, games had gone computer-crazy, and a new age of fads and gimmicks was in the making.

What's the hottest new game in America right now?

...00-year-old ...wling game ...om England.

Things look great in '68 for SKITTLE-BOWL, the game you couldn't get enough of last Christmas. Basic as bowling, with lasting appeal for all ages and both sexes, it takes skill to play, but even a pre-schooler can become a champ. Big and colorful. Features real wood pins, pole and ball. Bowling rules apply; but game variations are limitless. There's no end to the fun; Americans will be playing SKITTLE-BOWL BY AURORA for the next 400 years. The next best thing to having a bowling alley in your living room!

Item #5501   SKITTLE-BOWL GAME

AURORA PLASTICS CORP., 44 CHERRY VALLEY ROAD, WEST HEMPSTEAD, N.Y.
Aurora Plastics of Canada, 31 Racine Road, Rexdale, Ontario, Canada
Aurora Plastics Nederland N V, Nijverheidstat 15, Nijkerk, Holland
Aurora Plastics Co. UK Ltd., 64/70 High Street   Green Dragon House, Croydon   CR9   INA, England

The postwar years saw a lot of new developments in the toy field, as in the nation. One factor was growing sophistication on the part of toy buyers – parents. Kids, of course, were the real consumers, sometimes literally.

The war years had made big changes in traditional American mores. The rapid rise of television had a homogenizing effect on popular culture. Families clustered around their sets to see what TV personalities and families were talking about, wearing, laughing at, and buying. Then they did likewise. TV advertising brought undreamed-of results, and the toymakers were among the first to profit. Their messages to kids got instant replay to parents – "high reach and frequency," as the media people called it.

American educators looked glum when the Russians sent up the first satellite, *Sputnik*, in 1957. The race into scientific and space-oriented toys was on. "Earthside," such social scientists as Jean Piaget had offered new insights into cognitive development. This created a demand for toys that would not only entertain, but also enhance the skills and learning abilities of babies and preschoolers as well as older kids.

All these factors were at play in creating a new generation of toys, and kids didn't mind learning something from them if they served their main purpose – having fun.

One sign of the times was the Playskool Institute, founded by a former schoolteacher named Lucille King who was then working for the John Schroeder Lumber Company in Milwaukee. She wanted to bring out a line of wooden toys for preschool-age children, based on materials she had designed with a fellow teacher for classroom use. The lumber company agreed, and within a few years the two women had devised a line of some 40 products, including wooden beads, blocks, desks, dollhouses, pounding benches, and pegboards.

By the early 1960s, Playskool products were highly regarded and sold steadily to both parents and schools. Playskool Manufacturing was acquired by Milton Bradley in 1968. It is still turning out some of its earliest designs, including the Cobbler's Bench, which comes with six brightly colored pegs and a mallet. Toddlers hammer down the pegs on one side, then turn the toy over and do it again.

One of Playskool's longest-running favorites is its line of wooden blocks with safely rounded corners and edges. They have been offered as letter blocks, number blocks, and blocks with Disney, Sesame Street, and other characters on them. The sets range in contents from 16 to 50 natural wood-finish blocks, each $1\frac{5}{16}$ inches square. Each one has a picture embossed on two sides and printed on four sides. Originally sold in bags, they now come in sturdy canisters.

Playskool's Playtiles set was an advanced version of a pegboard, which enabled four-year-olds to create beautiful mosaic designs and pictures of random pattern by filling in the entire board. The sets came with 224 square, rectangular, and triangular tiles in four colors, which snapped securely onto the board.

LEFT: **Playskool's perennial wooden blocks, this set embossed with Disney characters. Who doesn't remember them?**

BELOW: **A Playskool puzzle that exemplified the Playskool Institute's theme of learning while playing.**

ABOVE: **Playskool's wooden workbench could keep a toddler busy pounding pegs for hours.**

LEFT: **This Playskool pull toy had an added advantage – stackable shapes.**

BELOW: **The quality of Playskool's wooden toys was enhanced by careful manufacturing, with many steps in production done by hand.**

In the early 1940s, Playskool acquired the Lincoln Logs firm from its founder, John Lloyd Wright. Appropriately, this popular construction toy had been devised by the son of America's most famous architect, Frank Lloyd Wright. Young Wright said he had gotten the idea in Tokyo while watching construction on his father's Imperial Hotel, which was designed to withstand earthquakes. He sold the first Lincoln Logs in 1916, and by 1975 the toy was still selling at the rate of a million sets per year.

With Lincoln Logs, you could make realistic cabins, ranches, forts, and bridges and people them with miniature frontiersmen and animals. The interlocking logs made a secure structure, and the flat green pieces could be used as roofing, tables, boundary lines and so forth. There was almost no better way to get through a rainy afternoon. The Pioneer Set came with 74 pieces, and the Scout Set had all of 90 pieces, including full logs, split logs, roof boards, gables and a chimney.

It's hard to believe now that it took Fisher-Price – founded in 1930 – six years to show a profit. But the firm not only weathered the Depression, it flourished. Is there anyone who grew up in the 1950s and 1960s without a Fisher-Price toy?

Now best known for its colorful, well-made plastic toys, Fisher-Price started out making quality wooden toys that were skillfully lithographed, designed mainly for children from six months to six years old. Herman Fisher and Irving Price had a major asset in Margaret Evans Price, Irving's wife, who was the company's first artist and designer. She had been a book and card illustrator, and her talent resulted in a variety of cheerful, colorful toys that were selling well when the United States entered World War II. Then, like many toymakers of the time, Fisher-Price became primarily a wartime industry. It manufactured ship fenders, first-aid kits, cots, bomb crates, and aircraft ailerons . . . a long way from the delightful

TOP LEFT: **Francesca and Andrew Charteris, British playmates of the young Prince Charles, with their Holgate block set in 1949.**

LEFT: **Two durable favorites from Fisher-Price – the Chatter Telephone and Pull-a-Tune Xylophone.**

ABOVE: **The original Lincoln Logs construction set, designed by architect J. L. Wright.**

TOP RIGHT: **Lincoln Logs were often imitated but were never equalled in popularity. The toy is still preserving the spirit of the wild frontier, for a new generation.**

Snoopy Sniffer pull toy introduced in 1938. More than four million of these felt-eared pups, from basset hounds to beagles, would be trundled around before the toy was retired in 1981.

By 1948, with postwar shortages of metal, rubber, and special woods behind it, Fisher-Price emerged as an industry leader. One of its most durable postwar creations was the Buzzy Bee – another engaging pull toy, with springy antennae, long-lashed eyes, and whirling wings. True to its name, it made a buzzing sound when pulled along by a captivated toddler. The Rattle Ball was pushed or dragged by a wooden rod attached to a plastic base filled with wooden balls that rattled when the toy moved. A similar concept – set to music – resulted in the perennial Musical Push Chime, still the longest-running toy in the Fisher-Price line.

The company's first all-plastic toy was This Little Pig, introduced in 1956. It was a string of small polyethylene pigs, similar in design to the colorful Snap-Lock Beads that came out the following year. A new generation is still gnawing happily on this indestructible toy.

Several manufacturers, including Emenee and Mattel, followed Fisher-Price's lead into the xylophone parade that began with the Teddy Bear Xilo in 1946. This colorful five-key toy evolved into the popular eight-key Pull-a-Tune Xylophone of the late 1950s, another long-playing classic of the innovative preschool line. Musical toys were big throughout the decade. Nineteen fifty-nine brought the Jack 'n' Jill TV-Radio, which combined a traditional Swiss music box that played nursery rhymes and a little screen that rotated images of the rhyme past the viewer while the tune was cranked out inside the "set." The Chatter Telephone came with a bell-ringing dial and sturdy plastic wheels that allowed the phone to function as a pull toy. Rolling eyes on the front of the base gave it a friendly expression.

ABOVE: **Squeaky the Clown, one of Fisher-Price's best-loved pull toys.**

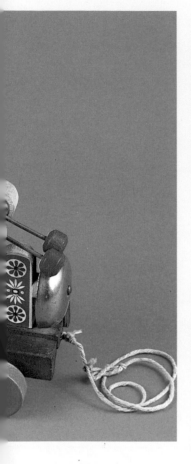

ABOVE: **Fisher-Price's bell-ringing rabbit, from the company's early days as a maker of wooden toys.**

RIGHT: **Musical Timmy Turtle kept up by moving his feet in time to the tune.**

The Safety School Bus included six removable figures that soon multiplied into a whole line of Play Family sets with their own houses, farms, hospitals, garages, airports, and more. The small people and pets are designed to sit securely in their furniture and vehicles.

Mattel was a new California company in the early 1950s, when it bought the rights to an invention that changed the future of musical toys. It was an unassuming rubber belt with bumps in it. When the belt moved, it struck prongs that played musical tunes, much like a player piano. Mattel made a number of successful musical instruments and preschool toys, including Hickory Dickory Clock, which played the familiar nursery tune of the same name while a mouse (of course) ran up the clock. Little organ grinders produced tunes at the turn of a crank, and even metal pets warbled when they were wound up.

Perhaps Mattel's best-known preschool toy was the inspired See 'n' Say series. These plastic noisemakers were imprinted with a wheel of images keyed to prerecorded sounds. You activated them by setting a pointer and pulling a drawstring. The Farmer Says set, with its loud, disembodied oinks, clucks, whinnys, and moos, was a particular favorite. Should your parents retain a tenuous grip on sanity under this barrage, you could turn on Mr. Sound Says, with its shrill assortment of trains, saws, and (appropriately) cuckoo clocks.

Another late 1960s favorite was the Mattel-O-Phone, with record discs that slid into the base. These contained short conversations with such celebrities as Cinderella, Santa Claus, and Barbie, the doll that built a fashion empire. By this time, Mattel's well-endowed teenage model was the uncrowned Miss America. (More about Barbie and her trendy friends and accessories in Chapter 3.)

The lithography company founded by Milton Bradley in the 1850s soon moved into the field of preschool toys and games. Bradley's father had been an admirer of Friedrich Froebel, the German advocate for kindergarten. Milton's education had been influenced by Froebel's methods, and in 1869 he published a book about them by Edward White entitled *Paradise of Childhood: A Practical Guide to Kindergartners*. Bradley's enthusiasm for early-childhood education led him to produce toys that could be used in kindergarten – tops, geometric shapes, simple games, and watercolors. His kindergarten line lost money for years, but Bradley never lost faith in it. At last, it began to pay off.

In the late 1960s, the Milton Bradley Company was among the first to recognize the value of "Sesame Street," the series produced by the non-profit Children's Television Workshop. Through the use of animation, puppets, and live characters, this now-classic series taught not only numbers and letters, but ways of exploring and working with children's feelings and concerns. The Sesame Street My First Games series became part of the Milton Bradley line.

Equally in demand were gaily colored figures of the show's best-loved characters: gregarious Bert and Ernie, gangling Big Bird, and the googly-eyed Cookie Monster, with his blue fur and white apron. By 1972 an unbelievable nine million Sesame Street toys were being liberated from toy stores by preschool kids and their approving parents.

When Hasbro (then Hassenfeld Brothers) introduced Mr. Potato Head in 1952, he really *was* a potato head. The funny assortment of plastic eyes, ears, noses, lips, hats, and pipes was designed to dress up a tuber

TOP: **The ultimate test for the Safety School Bus – holding up under a 170-pound Fisher-Price engineer.**

ABOVE: **Mr. Potato Head when he still had his pipe, which later fell victim to the antismoking brigade.**

TOP RIGHT: **Fisher-Price's Tot Toy Tribunal, which was observed through a one-way mirror.**

RIGHT: **The popularity of Mr. Potato Head inspired a whole line of produce that young creators could bring to life.**

LEFT: **The Danish firm of LEGO made its prewar toys of painted wood. These attractive samples are from about 1932.**

ABOVE: **LEGO System's Beginners' Set of jumbo plastic bricks appealed to tots.**

TOP: **With a LEGO set and a little imagination, the possibilities are endless.**

from the kitchen cupboard. Mr. Potato Head was the first toy to be advertised on television, and he helped make Hasbro what it is today – the biggest toymaker in the world. At this writing, the all-plastic version of the lumpy but lovable toy is still in demand. But by the late 1980s, Mr. Potato Head had lost his pipe to the antitobacco lobby.

The skyscraper of all the building toys, LEGO, originated in Denmark in the 1930s. Originally, the Christiansen family had made wooden toys, but their business expanded into plastic toys and building blocks during the postwar years. First there was a fish-shaped rattle for babies, then a tractor that could be put together and taken apart. In 1949, LEGO (from the Danish for "play well") introduced Automatic Binding Bricks, a forerunner of the familiar interlocking plastic blocks.

During the 1950s, LEGO moved to the current design and added accessories, including figures, wheels, and windows, in bright primary colors. LEGO was one toy that kids went back to again and again. You could make all kinds of structures, ships, trucks, planes – and the sets just got bigger and better. Now LEGO is sold all over the world, and it's hard to find a household with kids without a construction site at one stage of progress or another. The toy is almost indestructible and is often handed down to younger siblings or passed on to a family with younger kids.

A. C. Gilbert had been a leader in the educational toy field since 1913,

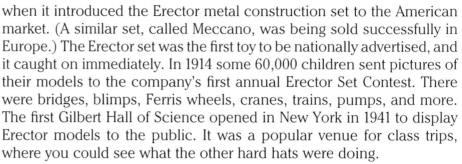

LEFT: **A. C. Gilbert's elaborate Erector sets brought out the best in aspiring engineers. National contests for the best model added the thrill of competition.**

ABOVE: **Wonderstruck, a scientist-in-the-making takes in an atomic laboratory set at the 1950 Toy Fair.**

when it introduced the Erector metal construction set to the American market. (A similar set, called Meccano, was being sold successfully in Europe.) The Erector set was the first toy to be nationally advertised, and it caught on immediately. In 1914 some 60,000 children sent pictures of their models to the company's first annual Erector Set Contest. There were bridges, blimps, Ferris wheels, cranes, trains, pumps, and more. The first Gilbert Hall of Science opened in New York in 1941 to display Erector models to the public. It was a popular venue for class trips, where you could see what the other hard hats were doing.

During the war years, the demand for metal meant that Erector sets had to be made of wood. Like so many others, the company turned to defense work, and did it well. But the postwar period brought record sales, and the introduction of remote control motors for various uses. The Electric Amusement Park Set enabled you to build a parachute jump and a Merry-Go-Round, and the Electric Engine Set produced an Airplane Ride and a Windmill that really turned. By 1953 some 30 million Erector sets had been sold.

A. C. Gilbert fell upon hard times during the 1960s; several expensive failures hastened its decline into bankruptcy. A series of takeovers ended in the Erector trademark going to Tyco Toys. However, a rejuvenated European Meccano acquired the Erector name from Tyco and introduced a new line of Erector sets to the American market in 1991. It looks like another building boom is underway.

During the late 1920s the Tinkertoy catalog overflowed with attractive toys made of brightly colored turned wood. Besides the Tinkertoy construction set itself, the company offered dolls, pull toys, beads, trains, animals, jump ropes, boats, tops, and Tinkerpins – a bowling game in which the pins were knocked down by a gyroscopic spinner. Over the next 25 years, Tinkertoy narrowed its line and updated its wooden building sets to include plastic wheels, connectors, and moving parts. The 1960s brought "space age models and added play possibilities" – still in the familiar tubular carton.

Playskool copied the Tinkertoy concept in its lookalike Makit Toy, which was offered as "a construction toy for the atomic age child five years to ten." Eventually, Playskool took over the manufacture of Tinkertoys. They're now more plastic than wood, but still colorful, well made, and fun for building everything from robots to rockets.

When Amsco brought out the elaborate Kidd-E-Doctor and Kidd-E-Nurse sets in the early 1950s it was the boys' kit, of course, that came with the impressive-looking doctor's diploma. But both sets were packed with true-to-life instruments, measuring devices, cotton balls, and real medical products like sterile gauze and Band-Aids from Johnson & Johnson. It was great value for $1.98, even at the time. And who knows how many of us ended up delivering babies or doing brain surgery as a result of this early exposure? Now Fisher-Price offers a unisex Medical Kit for tots to use on dolls, pets, and parents – complete with a blood-pressure cuff, reflex hammer, and hypodermic needle. Ouch.

A. C. Gilbert went to the head of the class again in the late 1950s with its impressive science kits for budding chemists, researchers, and nuclear physicists. Microscopes got more and more high-powered, and samples abounded in the Professional Microscope and Laboratory Set. If you ran out of exotic samples like shrimp eggs that hatched before your eyes,

LEFT: A. C. Gilbert's Lab Technician Set, for girls with a scientific bent.

BELOW: **This 1958 Erector set was for the junior engineer.**

RIGHT: **"Fun with Chemistry" started with an impressive set from A. C. Gilbert – 1952.**

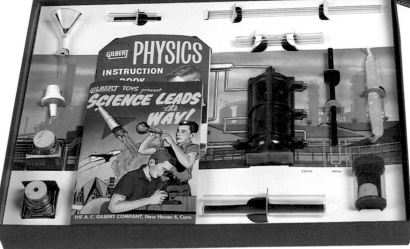

LEFT: Splitting the atom was child's play with a nuclear physics Atomic Energy Lab.

CENTER: The Gilbert microscope, with 60-90-210 magnification, was the centerpiece of this multi-purpose set.

ABOVE AND LEFT: The Fluid Dynamics Physics Set was a career-builder for hydropower enthusiasts.

47

TV's Mr. Wizard – Don Herbert – could show you how to do amazing experiments with stuff from the kitchen like vinegar and salt. Then came Gilbert's Atomic Chemistry Laboratory Set, designed to take you over the top into quantum physics ("Watch the disintegration of atomic particles!"). Fortunately, no one managed to duplicate the atomic bomb with this one.

Porter's Chemcraft line also had a high-tech Senior Lab Set for doing atomic experiments. According to the box, theirs even included "uranium ore"! The regular Chemcraft set wasn't too shabby either. It came with supplies and instructions for 750 experiments – all guaranteed harmless to life and limb. Porter's Microcraft set was intriguing to both future biologists and run-of-the-block kids fascinated by watching everyday worms, spiders, and ants turn into monsters under the powerful lenses of the microscope.

Even regular-size ants could be enthralling if you sent away for the underground ant city offered in the Edmund Scientific catalog. The glass sides of Edmund's Giant Ant Farm allowed you to see these busy little critters making tunnels, storing food, carrying eggs around, and what have you. Edmund Scientific also offered such natural wonders as crystal-growing and atomic-gardening kits. Other mail-order firms advertised in comic books and children's magazines such goodies as "Amazing Sea Monkeys," "Live Pet Seahorses," dinosaur bone collections, giant weather balloons, and more.

Future businessmen and -women of the early 1950s honed their skills on the popular Tom Thumb Typewriter and Cash Register, which were advertised as educational toys. Brumberger made a realistic Switchboard phone set, and a variety of walkie-talkies, telegraph sets, and amateur radio outfits enabled you to reach out and touch someone – at least to the other side of the yard.

Communications took another turn in the 1950s with View-Master's 3-D slide shows, featuring well-known TV and movie cartoon characters as well as reels on nature, travel, and famous events and people. When GAF took over this stereo slide scope, they created a Talking View-Master with a small record attached to the reels. The unit was back-lighted by a lamp or window.

Kenner offered a popular mixed-media set during the 1960s – an update of the old-time Magic Lantern. Their Give-a-Show Projector came with 112 color slides "giving 16 shows of TV favorites." These included the indestructible Popeye, near-sighted Mr. Magoo, bumbling Yogi Bear, hard-boiled Dick Tracy, Dennis the Menace, and even Lassie, the collie you just couldn't lose.

The educational toymakers had something for everyone during the heady boom years, and learning had never been more fun. We were supposed to grow up into "the best and the brightest," and if we didn't, we couldn't blame Playskool, Fisher-Price, or good old A.C. Gilbert.

The boom years also saw a burst of creativity in playthings and playtime. Children's natural fascination with color, shape, sound, and touch found new outlets as toymakers and television joined forces to inspire all kinds of skills and activities. These were halcyon days for getting up to your elbows in fingerpaints, Play-Doh, Colorforms, craft kits, coloring books, paint-by-number sets, and Plastigoop. It was all good fun, and if not clean, at least washable.

ABOVE: **Tinkertoys were a byword for creative play years before the company added plastic wheels, connectors, and moving parts. They're still fun, under the auspices of Playskool.**

TOP CENTER: **A 1980s version of Kenner's ever-popular Give-a-Show Theater.**

CENTER: **Creative Playthings were imaginative, well-designed, and safe for preschool children.**

ABOVE: **A Tom Thumb Cash Register was indispensable for totting up the proceeds from your lemonade stand.**

LEFT: **The GAF View-Master showed the Seven Wonders of the World and other educational subjects in 3-D Kodachrome. Reels of Casper the Friendly Ghost, and other TV and cartoon favorites, were almost as much fun to watch as the real thing.**

49

Creative Playthings caught the spirit of the times in offering toys designed to help develop a child's imagination. Founded in 1950 by Bernard Barenholtz and Frank Caplan, the company produced a line of simple, well-made vehicles in unpainted wood, smoothly finished: trucks, cars, planes, and trains. They symbolized the objects, rather than presenting them ready-made, as it were, allowing the child to "fill in the details" imaginatively. Creative Playthings were bought by preschools and kindergartens as well as by enthusiastic young parents who felt that elaborate toys and television might stunt their children's creativity.

Babies weren't neglected by the new and updated toymakers either. Creative Playthings produced a set of three soft plastic teethers in various textures and colors as a simple toy. They also offered a Baby Clutch Ball of soft rubber, with "handles" cut into the surface for easy grasping. Childcraft made a set of oversize cloth blocks that were easy for babies to stack and knock over without hurting themselves.

Stuffed animals had been around for a long time, but their play possibilities were extended in the postwar years. A more sophisticated public was concerned about toy safety, and the manufacturers turned increasingly to flame-resistant and washable materials. Standards grew stiffer with respect to nontoxic colors, nonshedding "fur," and secure attachment of eyes, ears, and other potentially detachable parts. Such venerable toys as the Teddy Bear and Winnie-the-Pooh were joined by a rainbow assortment of "stuffies" from the worlds of Walt Disney, Charles Schulz's "Peanuts" comic strip – Snoopy the beagle was a special favorite – and Sesame Street.

The German firm of Steiff had led the way into the field of sturdy, high-quality stuffed toys that could be passed down from one generation to the next. Then American manufacturers like Gund, founded in Connecticut in 1898 by Adolf Gund, became increasingly well known for the variety and appeal of their soft toys. Children had always formed strong attachments to their stuffed animals, and their value as playthings was enhanced by the many books, movies, and television shows that brought them to life for the younger child. Older children, including teenagers, loved to collect them as bedroom accessories – or so they said. But who knows whether they didn't give them a surreptitious hug now and then? Even some grown-ups have been known to do that in moments of stress. For now, at least, the future of stuffies seems assured.

Young dramatists and playwrights were inspired by toys such as the Disney Television Playhouse, new from Marx in 1953. The little theater itself was made of brightly lithographed metal, complete with painted footlights and a backdrop of scenes from *Dumbo, Pinocchio, Snow White and the Seven Dwarfs*, and other Disney animated-film classics. A variety of characters was made of soft, flexible vinyl plastic, and a tiny script gave you ideas for seven different dramas. Or you could make them up on your own.

Future Jackson Pollocks and Georgia O'Keeffes got a head start with a bewildering variety of art supplies, from the Crayola 64-pack crayon set from Binney & Smith to something called Lightning Bug Glo-Juice – a glow-in-the-dark paint introduced by Kenner in the late 1960s. Television's "Ding Dong School," presided over by Miss Frances (child psychologist Dr. Frances Horwich), gave rise to the official Ding Dong School Fingerpaint and Paintstiks sets, which were eagerly applied by

ABOVE: **In 1958 Binney & Smith added 16 new colors to its best-selling line of 48 Crayola crayons.**

RIGHT: **Painting by numbers was a great way to while away a rainy afternoon.**

PLAY SCHOOL WITH THE ROMPER ROOM COLORED PLASTIC "STICK-ONS". YOU'LL FIND THE TEACHER AND CHILDREN, MR. DO BEE, MR. DON'T BEE AND LOTS OF TOYS TO PUT ON THEIR PLACES IN THE SCHOOL ROOM. EVERYBODY ROMPS AND PLAYS. PRESS THE COLORFUL PLASTIC SHAPES WHERE YOU WANT THEM AND THEY'LL STICK LIKE MAGIC! TO MOVE, JUST LIFT THEM OFF, YOU CAN USE THEM AGAIN AND AGAIN. NO SCISSORS NEEDED. EVERYTHING IS PRE-CUT. IT'S THE NEATEST-EVER.

PLAY ROMPER ROOM SCHOOL ®

PLASTICONS ®

THE ROMPER ROOM

Mr. DO BEE T.M.

FAR LEFT: **Ready for the teddy bears' picnic – a rainbow assortment of the most popular stuffed toy ever.**

LEFT: **The popular "Romper Room" TV show for tots inspired a plastic stick-ons set with such characters as Mr. Do Bee and Mr. Don't Bee.**

BELOW: **Colorforms created a new dimension in play with its self-adhesive shapes for creating stories or patterns. This set was inspired by the 1967 Hollywood hit *Doctor Doolittle*.**

preschoolers to every available surface.

But the ultimate in art TV shows was Jack Barry's "Winky Dink and You." Winky Dink was a pixielike, big-eyed cartoon character who got you involved in his adventures through a "magic window" that stuck to the screen by static electricity. With certified Winky Dink "magic crayons," you could draw bridges, stairs, hide-outs, or what have you right on the TV screen to help Winky Dink escape pursuers, play tricks, or just generally raise hell. It could all be erased by the wipe of a "magic cloth" that came with the Winky Dink kit.

Another colorful innovation, which appealed to would-be fashion designers, was Kenner's Fashion Fun Sparkle Paints set. It came with a teenage paper doll named Sandy Sparkle and 10 up-to-the-minute outfits. You could dab the glittery colors on to taste and be part of the psychedelic world of the 1960s. This set was similar in concept to various Paint-A-Toy kits that had been marketed during the 1930s by companies like Soljertoy.

Watercolors sometimes produced disappointing results for the younger artist, who neglected to wash his or her brush before switching from one color to another. The result was a uniform muddy brown. Sanford addressed this problem with a set of six fluorescent watercolors in small bottles, already mixed and ready to use. The vibrant colors stayed clean and distinct.

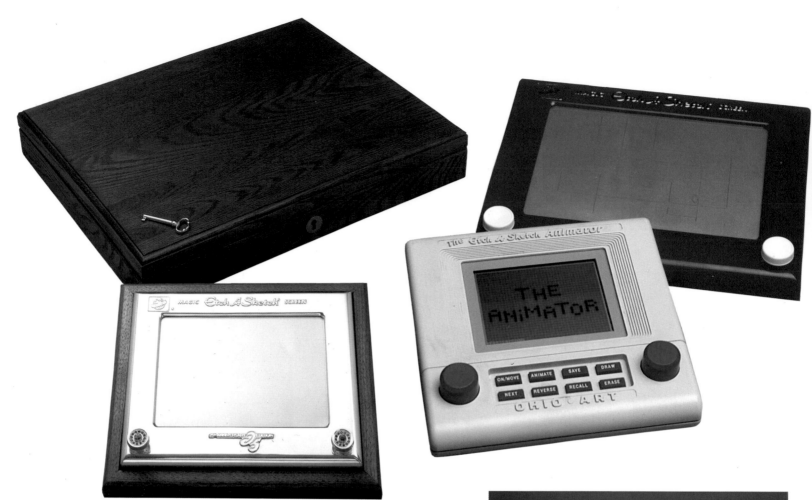

Another boon to the emerging artist was the development of brightly colored, precut, self-adhesive shapes that could be applied to printed backgrounds and other surfaces in endless recombination. Colorforms, of Norwood, New Jersey, was a pioneer in this new plaything, and Patterson Blick came out with a popular set called Play Shapes in various sizes. Easily dislodged from their backing sheets, these colorful vinyl pieces made great travel toys and inspired a rush to seal and sticker sets on such popular themes as flowers, dinosaurs, holidays, animals, and sport scenes.

Nineteen-sixty brought a creative toy that is still going strong 30 years later: Ohio Art's Etch A Sketch. The toy had been invented by a Frenchman named Arthur Grandjean and exhibited at the 1959 toy fair in Nuremberg, West Germany. Grandjean called it the Magic Screen. It consisted of a rectangular box with two knobs that were used to form letters, pictures, and other designs on the glass screen. When you turned it upside-down and shook it, the screen was blank again.

Ohio Art had some reservations about the toy – especially when the blueprints arrived with French instructions and metric measurements. But they pressed on and brought Etch A Sketch to market, with gratifying results. The toy was such a hit that the factory was assembling units until noon of the day before Christmas 1960 to meet the demand. When executives took the toy on business trips to New York, everyone on the plane wanted to play with it. Since then, some 50 million have been sold.

ABOVE: **With Ideal's Shaker Maker, you could create your own miniature hippie – love beads, sandals, and all.**

RIGHT: **Hasbro's illuminated pegboard, Lite-Brite, was an immediate and enduring success.**

FAR LEFT: **The 25th Anniversary edition of Ohio Art's Etch A Sketch, with walnut case and frame and jewelled knobs.**

LEFT: **At top, the original Etch A Sketch; below, the Animator version for "cartoonists" in search of action art.**

RIGHT: **Kids were enthralled by Kenner's Spirograph, which enabled them to draw complex designs to perfection.**

For the 25th anniversary of Etch A Sketch, in 1985, Ohio Art produced an executive model in which the plastic border was replaced by walnut, trimmed with silver and jewels. This was not surprising, since the company had been making picture frames successfully since the turn of the century. Now Etch A Sketch can be purchased in an electronic version that animates your drawings. But the original "Magic Screen" is still the most popular.

Another enduring visual-art toy of the 1960s was Kenner Products' Spirograph, which enabled you to draw unlimited designs in psychedelic colors through a combination of gears, discs, and pens. At the time, Spirograph was advertised as a toy for all ages. It still is, although today's marketing is directed towards kids of five and up. Some 30 million Spirographs have been sold since they were introduced in the mid-1960s.

Lite Brite was essentially an electronic peg board with which you could "draw" objects in colored light by inserting the pegs into a precut paper pattern. When the paper was peeled away – *Voila!* A running horse in living color! Or whatever else you chose to design. This imaginative toy has long outlived fad status to become a classic for a new generation.

Rainbow Crafts introduced the indestructible Play-Doh in 1955, in response to the need for a modeling material that was cleaner and easier to handle than clay and that didn't dry out after sitting around awhile. Preschoolers took Play-Doh to their hearts, and parents bought it by the truckload. It was an easy clean-up and could be used again and again.

53

Rainbow Crafts soon expanded the line into four colors, and it didn't hurt that Play-Doh was advertised on the perennial "Beany and Cecil" television show, which had been around since the late 1940s. The ebullient Beany and his friends, including the engaging Cecil (the Seasick Sea Serpent), old-timer Pop Gunn, adventurous Horatio Huffenpuff, and the mildly menacing Dishonest John were a fixture on children's television until the mid-1960s. Originally, they were hand puppets created by Bob Clampett for the 1949 show "Time for Beany." The puppet show ran through 1954, and the color cartoon series began in 1962. It launched a series of popular hand puppets, stuffed toys, helicopter beanies, talking dolls, boats modeled on Beany's *Leakin' Lena*, and even a Cecil Jack-in-the-Box from Mattel.

Play-Doh was acquired by Kenner, which had been formed in 1947 by the Steiner brothers, Al, Phil, and Joe, on Kenner Street in Cincinnati.

ABOVE LEFT: **Play-Doh was a boon both to would-be sculptors and to those who cleaned up their studios.**

LEFT: **Ideal's Shape & Play Workbench used a modelling material similar to Play-Doh.**

ABOVE: **Play-Doh invaded the kitchen with molds and utensils that converted the versatile stuff into look-alike turkeys, cakes, and other mock edibles.**

Have Fun!

Everyone from Junior to Grandpa will get a kick out of creating "Kritters" — Keep the children scrap-happy with a Kritter Club! Give a hilarious Kritter-making party for grown-ups! Make your own amusing prizes and table decorations! This kit contains all the materials necessary for making a flock of them, with photographs and complete instructions.

R KIT

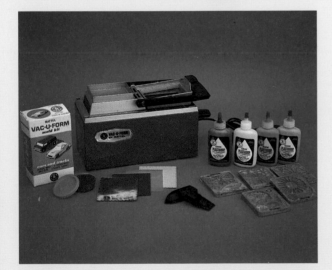

TOP: **The Kritter Kit started the trend toward make-it-yourself monsters.**

ABOVE: **With Mattel's Vac-U-Form heating element, a selection of molds and a supply of Plastigoop, you could make lots of neat things. When the Vac-U-Form became the Thingmaker, and the molds made Creepy Crawlers and Incredible Edibles, Mattel hit the jackpot.**

Twenty years later, the firm was taken over by General Mills, but Play-Doh is still marketed under the Kenner name, with a variety of colorful molds and accessories licensed by Disney, including the Disney Duck Tales Play-Doh play set. Earlier sets had included the popular Play-Doh Factory and Kitchen, which enabled you to turn out Play-Doh creations at assembly-line speed.

Monsters had been popular since the 1950s, when a host of science-fiction movies raised the specter of mutation through atomic radiation in pictures like *THEM!*, *The Thing,* and *Attack of the Crab Monsters*. Kids had always loved being scared to death, and in the 1960s they could do it themselves with Mattel's Plastigoop, molded into various frightful forms by an electric heating element called the Thingmaker. Mattel took the concept to the limit with toys like Creeple Peeple, Creepy Crawlers, and the Batman Bat-Maker Pak. Should these pall, the company produced a Fright Factory with which you could make such ghoulish items as fangs, claws, bloodshot eyes, and scars in which to dress up and terrify your friends. The denouement was a kit called Incredible Edibles, which featured an almost-palatable version of Plastigoop that you could mold into bugs, snakes, caterpillars and so forth and then consume. Gross!

More conventional craft kits could be obtained from Lisbeth Whiting, which produced nothing more alarming than Oscar the Octopus, made of yarn. His braided legs were tied off with ribbon, and he sported a small hat and a friendly expression. Funny Face Pot Holders made a great homemade (and free) gift for your mother, and boys could be induced to produce a tile ashtray or two. Another Lisbeth Whiting favorite was the Mosaic Tile Candy Dish, closely followed by the Lazy Susan. The Fun with Sticks kit was sold as a unisex item – girls and their brothers could get involved in making stuff out of recycled popsicle sticks.

The sound of music was not neglected by baby boom toymakers like Colmor, Emenee, Hezzie, and the Jefferson guitar company. Kids were encouraged to express themselves musically on everything from the Hezzie Junior Slide Whistle to the Spike Jones Junior City Slickers drum set from Colmor. Both these toys had a high nuisance value, but parents didn't want to stifle creativity so they suffered through the cacophony as long as they could.

Emenee produced a comparatively melodious xylophone, touted on television by plaid-suited Pinky Lee, a former burlesque star who hosted a popular children's show in the 1950s. The four-string Emenee cowboy guitar featured Western film star Gene Autry, at home on the range. Creative Playthings marketed a Rhythm Band Set that had six percussion instruments, including a tambourine, cymbals, wood tone block, and castanets. This definitely offered more bang for the buck.

The 1955 *Toy Yearbook* featured a variety of popular musical toys, including Hill bell toys, a Schoenhut grand piano, and several Emenee plastic instruments. Colorful Melodé Bells came with color-coded music sheets that showed you how to ring the eight-bell sets, which embodied the tones of the major scale. The Jefferson guitar company offered a host of enameled-cardboard models emblazoned with motifs designed to appeal to kids: By the Sea, Palomino Pony, the Lone Ranger, and, in the early 1960s, the Twist model, tuned to the latest dance fad. With the accompanying book of chords, it was possible to plunk out something resembling a tune.

ABOVE: **Danish immigrant and inventor Finn Haakon Magnus made his fortune in plastic musical instruments for children.**

TOP RIGHT: **A. C. Gilbert's Lite-a-Tune Piano made learning the scale an illuminating experience.**

RIGHT: **A Gene Autry guitar from Emenee was essential for musical cowpokes around an imaginary campfire.**

LEFT: **A. C. Gilbert's Mysto Magic Show set was at least as entertaining as the company's better-known science kits, and it was great at parties.**

Jefferson Guitars for the Hootenanny Stars

HOOTENANNY GUITAR
No. H-4 CORAL

ROY ROGERS GUITAR
No. 70 BROWN

LENGTH 30''
DEPTH 3¼''
WIDTH 11''
2½ lbs. each

No. X60 SPECIAL 4-STRING GUITAR MAHOGANY

LENGTH 30''
DEPTH 3¼''
WIDTH 11''
2½ lbs. each

LENGTH 24''
DEPTH 2½''
WIDTH 9½''
1¾ lbs. each

SPECIAL
No. 80
6-STRING GUITAR MAHOGANY

HAWAIIAN GUITAR
No. 72 CORAL

LENGTH 30''
DEPTH 3¼''
WIDTH 11''
2½ lbs. each

LENGTH 3
DEPTH 3
WIDTH
2½ lbs. e

Rock 'n' roll inspired a new wave of musical merchandise that began with the Elvis Presley doll and the first electric guitar for kids and crested in Beatlemania, which hit American shores from the U.K. in 1964. The advent of the four mop-topped mods from Liverpool brought with it not only multimillion-dollar record sales, but an advertising and merchandising blitz of mythic proportions. Not only were there Beatles toy guitars, banjos, trap drum sets, and bongos – there were Beatles lunchboxes, sneakers, buttons, wallets, jewelry, glasses, tote bags, outfits, wigs, and more.

Fifth Avenue looked more like Carnaby Street every day, as mod British fashions took over Saks Fifth Avenue and Bloomingdale's chic new boutiques. The faces of John, Paul, George, and Ringo were more familiar to American kids than the presidential profiles carved on Mount Rushmore. The music world would never be the same again, and teenaged baby boomers were the Pied Pipers who would call the tune into another decade.

FAR LEFT: **Jefferson Guitars came in vivid designs and colors, from the Roy Rogers model to the swaying palms of the Hawaiian Holiday model.**

BELOW LEFT: **Beatles dolls (this set with nodding heads) were the icon of a generation.**

BELOW: **Modelmaker Revell got on the Beatles bandwagon with a set of make-your-own moptops.**

BOTTOM: **Blow-up Beatles in inflatable vinyl took Beatlemania over the top.**

In the postwar era, before the women's movement raised our consciousness, the strongest claim you could make for a girl's toy was that it was "just like Mom's!" Miniature versions of Mom's kitchen set, carpet sweeper, cleaning supplies, and baby-care items poured into the marketplace for the millions of little girls who were, presumably, housewives in training.

A lot of the new technology landed on toy shelves in the form of little coffee pots that made realistic burbling sounds (Amsco's Wonder Perk) and lightweight aluminum cookware scaled down to child size by Mirro. The reliable Amsco (short for American Metal Specialties Corp.) also came up with the Little Queen Bissell Sweeper Set and everything you could need for a play nursery, including a Wonder Sterilizer and the Doll-E line of furnishings. Doll-E could provide you with a scaled-down crib, highchair, nurser, bassinette, and swing, not to mention a Cry Baby Magic Bottle. It let out a crying noise when the doll was "drinking" and stopped when the feeding was over. When dolls learned how to wet as well as drink, Amsco was ready, with the Doll-E-Pottychair.

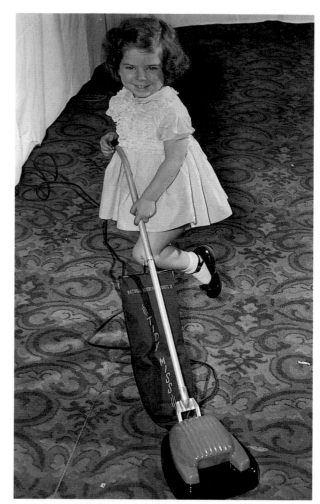

Like Amsco, Norstar had tie-ins with many manufacturers of adult products, which were repackaged for play sets. Norstar's Little Handi-Aid cleaning sets came complete with little packs of Bab-O Cleanser and Brillo pads, plus mops, brooms, dusters, aprons and everything else you needed to polish up your housekeeping skills.

Once you got the playhouse cleaned up, you could turn on your toy stove and produce a culinary masterpiece – real or imaginary. Toy stoves could be as simple as a cardboard cutout with plastic knobs or as elaborate as the colorful enameled-steel model from Gabriel Nassau. If your house – or your dad's bank account – were big enough, you could get a whole Little Miss Nassau kitchen, with a refrigerator as big as you were (freezer included), a sink, an oven, and cabinets to match. (The Gabriel company was expanding all over the place at the time. When it wasn't making appliances, it was buying up A. C. Gilbert, including Erector sets.)

Even better than real-looking toy ovens were those that actually baked something, like Kenner's 1962 Easy-Bake Oven. Light bulbs were the heating source – safe, but slow. Easy-Bake came with tiny Betty Crocker cake and cookie mixes "just like Mom's." Somehow, the finished products always looked better on television, but the real fun was mixing the stuff up and pouring it into the little pans. Easy-Bake is still around, but now, of course, it's a microwave.

Junior Chef was a strong contender in the toy appliance market, with its See It Bake Oven, Poppity Popper for pint-size servings of popcorn, Tasty Custard Maker, and even a Cotton Candy Machine. Now you could produce that sumptuous, airy stuff you bought at the amusement park right at home, provided you had enough sugar to make all your fillings fall out.

Although better known for its boys' toys, like Johnny Lightning Jet Power Cars, Topper Toys got into the great American bake-off with a line

LEFT: Vacuum cleaning when it was fun – with a Tidy Miss sweeper demonstrated at the 1949 New York Toy Fair.

RIGHT: Amsco's detailed Doll-E-Toys were a delight for playing house, when Kidd-E-Doctors and Nurses still made house calls.

BOTTOM LEFT: The Kiddie Training Sink held hot and cold water for five wash-ups before its tank ran dry.

See how easy it is to feed dolly in this sturdy metal hichair! It's so big and beautifully decorated—stands 30" high. **DOLL-E-HICHAIR $3.98***
Other hichairs from $1.69

Make the formula . . . sterilize the bottles . . . Everything needed for dolly's feeding is here in authentic miniature. . . . . . . De Luxe 32-piece **DOLL-E-FEEDER $2.98***
Other formula sets from $1.00

Playing doctor and nurse is more fun than ever with Amsco's medical kits, fully equipped even to actual Johnson & Johnson products. Every one of the 63 authentic items has real educational and play value. **KIDD-E-DOCTOR** or **KIDD-E-NURSE $1.98***

For Sister's very best dolly . . . Amsco's beautiful metal crib with washable plastic mattress. It's 26" long and realistic in every detail from adjustable dropside to swivel casters. . . . . **DOLL-E-CRIB $9.95***
Other cribs and cradles from $7.49

they love to play "grown up" with **Amsco® DOLL-E-TOYS**
DURABLE · EDUCATIONAL
At Leading Toy Counters Coast-to-Coast!
American Metal Specialties Corporation, Hatboro, Penna.

Little Mommy loves dolly's bunkbeds—finds it fun to separate them into twin beds, too. Sturdy steel, 26" long, with mattresses and ladder . . . . . **DOLL-E-BUNKBEDS $12.95***
Other beds from $1.98

A real bath for dolly in a leakproof plastic tub. Doll-E-Bath is equipped with soap, washcloth and every baby bathing accessory. Sturdy steel frame prevents tipping. . . . . . **DOLL-E-BATH $4.98***
Other baths from $3.98

Of course dolly's dishes sparkle! With Amsco's complete dishwashing set, little Mommy has *everything* she needs, including filled packages of Ajax, Vel, Brillo; and Cadie Cloth. Gift-packed. . . . . . . **DOLL-E-DODISH $1.98***
Prices vary slightly in some sections

LEFT: Mirro's battery-operated Pla-Vac set featured the popular Campbell kids of soup-commercial fame.

RIGHT: Kenner's Easy-Bake Oven was among the most-wanted toys of the 1962 holiday season.

BELOW: The Micro-Mix set from Micromatic Tool & Manufacturing was one of those mini-appliances that worked "just like Mother's."

BOTTOM RIGHT: The Suzy Homemaker Mixer from Topper appealed to the universal instinct for stirring things up.

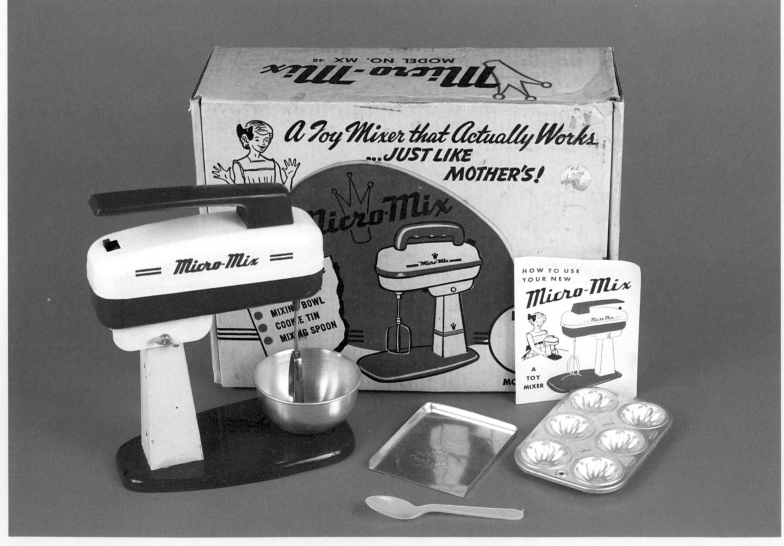

of appliances called Suzy Homemaker. Topper's 1966 Super Oven could make bigger cakes than Kenner's Easy Bake, and package-goods producers were standing in line to turn out miniature mixes for future shoppers. Well-known brands like Flako, Swan's Down, Aunt Jemima, Log Cabin, and Chef Boy-Ar-Dee were staples in the toy kitchen as well as in the real one. Kay Van offered reasonably priced Small Fry Cooking Sets made of "pure aluminum" with which to stir up, bake, and fry all these groceries.

After Mattel's big success with the monstrous Incredible Edibles, perhaps it was inevitable that the California company would enter the toy-kitchen sweepstakes with something called Kooky Kakes. The concept was similar to that of Incredible Edibles: a round metal heating element and a supply of batter (called Gobbledegoop) in tubes. TV advertising did the rest.

Although Mattel targeted both boys and girls as creators of Kooky Kakes, it's likelier that the boys consumed more than they baked. At the time, most Little Leaguers weren't planning to become Mr. Mom when they grew up. (Some would later change their minds under duress from disgruntled Suzy Homemakers.)

TEA SETS

No. 407
"TEA TIME" TEA SET
Lithoed metal and plastic.
Window box package.
2 doz. ctn. Approx. wt. 18 lbs.

No. 409
Time for Tea
Lithoed metal.
Window box package.
1 doz. ctn. Approx. wt. 12 lbs.

No. 420
Swiss Miss
TEA SET
Lithoed metal.
Complete service for 4.
Window box package.
1 doz. ctn. 23 lbs.

No. 402
Play time TEA SET
Lithoed metal.
Blister package.
2 doz. ctn. 7 lbs.

No. 397 MECHANICAL METAL TOASTER
Lithoed metal. 7½" x 4¾" x 5".
1 doz. ctn. 9½ lbs.

No. 440 **Red Riding Hood** TEA SET
Lithoed metal and plastic. Complete service for 4 plus goblets, sherbets and silverw...
Fruit bowl and realistic fruit made in Hong Kong. Tray size: 13¾" x 10⅜".
Full color "book style" box permits easy stacking. Easy to open and stand for dis...
½ doz. ctn. 22½ lbs.

NO. 400 "BO PEEP" TEA SET
Six pieces. 4 colors.
Metal lithoed. 2 plates,
2 cups, 2 saucers.
3 doz. ctn. 12 lbs.

NO. 402 "HAWAIIAN FLORAL" TEA SET
BLISTER PACKAGE.
7 Pieces. 4 color lith-
oed metal. 2 each;
cups, saucers, 4" plates.
One 5¼" round serv-
ing plate.
2 doz. ctn. 9½ lbs.

ABOVE: **Ohio Art set an elegant tea table with its colorful metal-litho sets.**

TOP RIGHT: **The "Tracy" doll, seen here at the Brighton, England, Toy Fair, specialized in pouring tea and handing around cakes.**

CENTER: **Ohio Art's 1963 catalog featured a 35-piece Holiday Partyware set handsome enough to grace the dinner table.**

RIGHT: **GW's toy Bar-Bee-Q looked just like the one in the backyard, but it worked on flashlight batteries instead of charcoal.**

64

While it was mainly British girls who grew up to give tea parties, American girls had been playing with tea sets since colonial times. Most of them were imported from England or the Continent, if they weren't handmade at home. But by 1850, the U.S. census listed dozens of domestic toymakers, most of whom were producing painted tin toys. These "tin men," as they were called, are inseparable from the history of American toymaking.

Ohio Art began making lithographed tin tea sets after World War I. Other companies produced the popular playthings in china, glass, ceramic, and later, plastic and aluminum. During the postwar era, Creative Playthings came up with a sturdy 17-piece aluminum tea set that included four cups, saucers, and plates along with a covered teapot, sugar bowl, and creamer. The place settings were big enough to accommodate real, as well as "make-pretend," snacks. Creative Playthings also offered a set of durable knives, forks and spoons, plus baking and other cookware.

Late in the 1960s, Chilton came up with a line of tea sets and aluminum cookware, including the Qualitea Sets, which had plastic copies of the popular Corning Ware line. None of these innovations could displace my personal favorite: an old-fashioned china tea set in the classic Blue Willow pattern that appeared under the Christmas tree in the early 1950s. My sister got an identical set, so we could give tea parties worthy of a prime minister – at least in terms of the number in attendance.

Although better known in the mid-1960s for its G.I. Joe action figure, Hasbro didn't neglect the home front. Its Frosty Sno-Cone Maker was an immediate hit with both genders. Another hot-weather favorite was

NO. 426 "HOLIDAY" PARTYWARE SET
Beautiful 35 piece plastic and metal Holiday set with large 13½" x 18½" metal tray. 4 polystyrene goblets, 4 polystyrene sherbets, and 4 each: metal plates, cups, and saucers. Polyethylene creamer and sugar. 4 each: polystyrene knives, forks, spoons. Exceptionally attractive package hinges for easy counter display.
½ doz. ctn. 22½ lbs.

NO. 401 "TEA FOR TWO" TEA SET
Complete set of seven pieces. 2 cups, 2 saucers, 2 4" plates, 1 (5⅛" round) serving plate. Lithoed metal.
2 doz. ctn. 16 lbs.

NO. 410 "BLUE HEAVEN" TEA SET
WINDOW BOX PACKAGE. 15-piece set. Metal lithoed in 4 colors. 4 each: dinner plates, cups, saucers, 1 (8" x 10") tray, 1 creamer.
1 doz. ctn. 19 lbs.

407 "MISS PETITE" TEA SET
WINDOW BOX PACKAGE. 13-piece 4 each: dinner plates, cups, saucers, (5¼" x 7½")tray. Metal lithoed colors.
2 doz. ctn. 22½ lbs.

Kenner's Freeze Queen soft ice cream maker, complete with cones and recipes. The Whiz Fizz Soda Fountain from Kenner dispensed soft drinks made from colored powder in three flavors. Topper's entry in the race for hyperglycemia was a candymaker called Sweet Shops.

By the late 1960s you could even have a barbecue with Kenner's Big Burger Grill – powered by a single light bulb. And Amsco had come out with the Wonder Corn Popper, which produced an energetic popping noise and not much else – without winding or batteries. Throughout the decade, toymakers had labored successfully to give new meaning to the phrase "small appliance."

One very old plaything that got a whole new look in the postwar years was the dollhouse, both plain and fancy. Dollhouses came to America by way of Europe and Great Britain, where they were called "baby houses" from the eighteenth century on. In Europe, dollhouses had been primarily showcases for fine miniatures, but the British dollhouses were made to be played with. Some of the best known include the late seventeenth-century cabinet house given to Ann Sharp by her godmother, the future Queen Anne, and the stately Georgian baby house at Uppark, in Dorset, which belonged to Sarah Lethieullier.

Lacquered furniture and wax or wooden dolls were commercially made and sold in British toy stores for the less ornate dollhouses of the average child. Many families crafted their own furniture and sewed tiny linens and hangings for the houses. Apparently, little brothers were as big a problem then as they would be later. A dollhouse of the Regency period bears the painted notice: "Warning. Boys throwing stones against the back of this house will be prosecuted with the utmost severity!"

TOP LEFT: **A postwar "dream house" of the popular metal-litho type with traditional furnishings.**

ABOVE: **Marx's delightful metal-litho dollhouse was easy to assemble and filled with the realistic details that made Marx toys so desirable.**

RIGHT: **A modular dollhouse living room in contemporary style.**

FAR RIGHT: **Modular dining room complete with framed artwork and chandelier.**

The earliest known American dollhouse is dated 1744. It was built in the Dutch cabinet style for a child of the Homan family in Boston. In 1895 the Bliss Manufacturing Company of Pawtucket, Rhode Island, introduced attractive wooden houses with colorful lithographed-paper decorations. The company advertised them as "American designs to suit the taste of American children."

By the early twentieth century, F.A.O. Schwartz was offering dollhouses lit by electricity at its Fifth Avenue shop. Albert Schoenhut advertised "Artistic high class doll's houses and bungalows" that ranged from one-roomers to eight-room mansions. Little shrubberies were available for landscaping the front garden of the mansion models.

Tootsietoy dollhouses and furnishings were first offered during the 1920s, including an elegant Spanish house and a mansion made of heavy book board. Tootsietoy's furniture was proclaimed to have "All the strength of metal, all the beauty of wood." Like Ohio Art, Mattel had started out making picture frames, then turned to making toy furniture from the leftover scraps of wood and plastic. The company was successful from the start, although it faced a setback with the advent of injection-molded doll furniture at lower prices. Owners Ruth and Elliott Handler quickly diversified into toy musical instruments, which saved the day.

The most popular dollhouses of the baby boom years were contemporary-style models in lithographed metal, peopled and furnished in plastic. Most of the metal dollhouses were sold flat, but assembled readily by bending tabs into prepunched holes. Happi Time offered a two-story house with a nursery and master bedroom upstairs and a recreation room attached to the house by a breezeway. It looked just like the suburban houses that sprang up like mushrooms after World War II. So did Marx's T-shaped ranch house, which bore little resemblance to its frontier forebears.

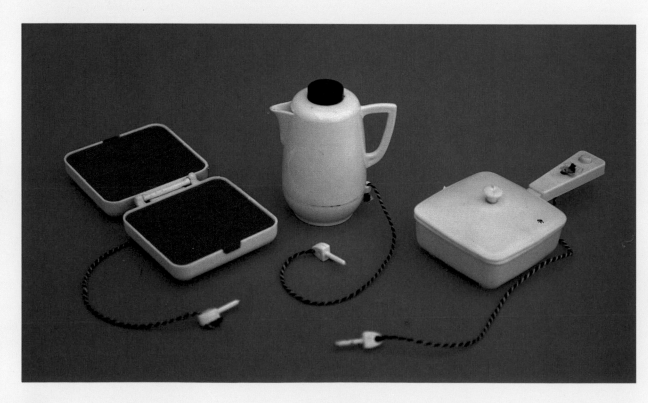

ABOVE: **Disney-licensed toys from the studio's animated-film classics were a boon to manufacturers. Lucky was the little girl who had the Snow White Kitchen Set.**

LEFT: **"General Electric Kitchen" mini waffle iron, coffee pot, and frying pan, for the dollhouse kitchen.**

RIGHT: **Structo Toys' dollhouse-sized GE appliances included this range and sink unit.**

FAR RIGHT: **A multicolored dream kitchen for the dollhouse, by Deluxe Toys.**

The uniformly pink doll families that came with the houses ranged in size from four to fourteen members (including a cat). As in earlier days, you could also buy larger-scale individual rooms, with eight-inch dolls to match. Children's imagination and enduring fascination with miniatures prevailed over all the vicissitudes of dollhouse taste and fashion. Some long-grown girls are still happily playing with dollhouses – only now they call themselves collectors.

The theme song of postwar toymakers must have been "Oh, You Beautiful Doll," judging by the incredible variety and volume of dolls and accessories that hit the market in the 1950s. Dolls had been less affected by wartime shortages than other toys, as they had long been made of composition – essentially, glue and sawdust. Mary Had a Little Lamb and other popular toys in the Story Book Doll series weathered the war years, and so did rag doll toys like Raggedy Ann and Andy.

Raggedy Ann was the creation of political cartoonist Johnny Gruelle, who was working for the *Indianapolis Star* in 1915, when his daughter Marcella contracted tuberculosis. To entertain her, Gruelle found a handmade rag doll in his attic, which he named Raggedy Ann, from the James Whitcomb Riley characters "The Raggedy Man" and "Little Orphan Annie." Then he made up stories about the doll. He published the stories in 1917, after Marcella's death, with copies of the doll. Soon Raggedy Andy, too, was being manufactured by the P. F. Volland Company, which published the stories. Despite the sad circumstances of their origin, these round-eyed, carrot-topped dolls are still exerting their charm on a new generation.

LEFT: **Madame Alexander dolls such as this Little Women set of Meg, Jo, Beth, and Amy, were beautifully designed and costumed.**

BELOW LEFT: **All-time favorites Raggedy Ann and Andy – "America's Folk Dolls."**

FAR LEFT: **The exquisite Caroline doll, a 1961 addition to the Madame Alexander line.**

RIGHT: **The ever-popular Kewpie in the 1970s, from Jesco Doll Co.**

BELOW: **The 1950 Kewpie doll, with its familiar dimpled knees and curly topknot.**

RIGHT: **Ideal's Shirley Temple doll evoked memories of Hollywood's favorite child star.**

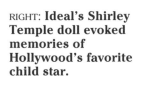

LEFT: **Almost-lifesize Kissy puckered up and kissed back when her arms were lifted.**

RIGHT: **The long-running "I Love Lucy" show reprised in a paper doll set with Lucille Ball, Desi Arnez, and Little Ricky.**

LEFT: **Tiny Tears came with her own package of Kleenex.**

Another perennial doll is the Kewpie, a cherubic tot with a curl on top of his (or her) head. The character was created by illustrator Rose O'Neill for the *Ladies' Home Companion* in 1909 and became a popular feature. So many people wanted Kewpie as a doll that O'Neill advertised for someone to design one, and Joseph Kallus, then studying sculpture at Brooklyn's Pratt Institute, took on the job. At first, the dolls were manufactured in Germany and imported to the United States. Then Kallus formed the Cameo Doll company to make them himself. Since 1969 Kewpies have been licensed to several manufacturers, most recently to Jesco, and their place in popular culture seems secure.

Shirley Temple had brightened the Depression years as a child star of unprecedented popularity, and she wasn't forgotten in the postwar years – especially by Ideal Corporation. The grown-up Shirley Temple helped sell the many Ideal versions of her image as the perfect American girl. All

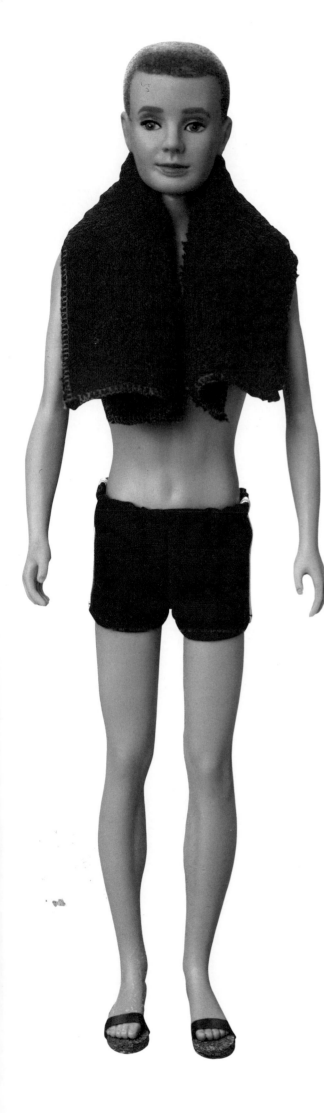

the Shirley Temple dolls had curly hair, white anklets, big eyes, and sweet expressions. You almost expected them to go into a tap dance or start singing "The Good Ship Lollipop," but doll technology hadn't gotten that far yet.

Ideal's baby dolls of the 1950s comprised a nurseryful of toys that required almost as much care as real infants and toddlers. They drank from bottles, wet, opened and closed their eyes, took baths, cried, kissed, walked, fell down, rolled over, grew hair, and waved bye-bye. Ideal was just as inventive with their names. Who can forget Betsy Wetsy, Bye Bye Baby, Rub a Dub Dolly, Tiny Tears, Wake-up Thumbelina, Kissy, or Judy Splinters? Actually, Judy Splinters was licensed by Ideal from the early children's show of the same name. Talented puppeteer Shirley Dinsdale had created the three-foot-high ventriloquist doll, who looked like a child of four, to appear with another appealing puppet called Lamb Chop who was, not surprisingly, a lamb. The show won two well-deserved Emmys during the late 1940s and early 1950s, when all shows were done live. (Remember the great Kate Smith singing "When the Moon Comes Over the Mountain" at the end of her program? And Jimmy Durante's famous sign-off: "Good night, Mrs. Calabash, wherever you are"? They don't make TV stars like that any more.)

Then it was 1959, and the doll market was revolutionized – by Barbie. Innovative Mattel Inc. had been working on a teenage doll for several years, partly because Ruth and Elliott Handler's daughter Barbie was paying more attention to fashion paper dolls than to baby dolls. And so were a lot of other preteens.

According to Barbie's biographer, fashion designer BillyBoy, the original Barbie doll was based on a German line called Lilli dolls, tied to a comic strip. Mattel bought the rights to Lilli, who was slender, long-legged, seductive-looking – and stacked. When her American cousin was introduced at the 1959 Toy Fair, eyebrows shot up. Toy buyers weren't sure American girls – or their parents – were ready for Barbie. However, as the toy reached the stores, Barbie started looking better to the trade. Initial shipments sold out, and the demand for Barbie and her stylish outfits became clamorous.

Barbie was everything the nascent teenager wanted to be. "She's curvy and life-like, and she stands alone," proclaimed Mattel. Even better was her wardrobe ("authentic in every detail!"), which included spike heels, swimsuits, shorty pajamas, sailing outfits, form-fitting pants, evening gowns, hoop earrings, elegant accessories – and bras. The clothes were meticulous, with working zippers, well-turned cuffs, and silk linings. Mattel had contracted with a Japanese company to make Barbie's clothes at a price far lower than it would have been in the United States. This was one of the first instances in which American toymakers turned to the Far East for high-quality, affordable goods, and the relationship paid off handsomely.

FAR LEFT: **The original Mattel Barbie doll in the 1959 debut.**

LEFT: **The Ken doll appeared in 1961 looking slightly aenemic. In time he became more robust.**

LEFT: **Members of the wedding: Barbie's best friend Midge and long-haired flower girl Skipper (1964).**

BELOW: **Barbie and Skipper meticulously clad in their red velvet dress coats and accessories.**

LEFT: **Mattel designers are attuned to haute couture at home and abroad in creating the sumptuous wardrobes for Barbie and her friends.**

BELOW: **Sign of the times: Christie, Barbie's black friend, was introduced in 1968.**

To this day, Mattel sends designers to fashion shows by top couturiers around the world to keep Barbie dressed in the style to which she's accustomed. Meanwhile, of course, she's acquired a host of friends and relations, from bland-looking Ken to Julia, a black doll based on the character played by Diahann Carroll in the late-1960s series of the same name. Ken ("He's a doll!") looked like the kind of boy parents prayed their daughters would go out with. Of course, he needed clothes too, and so did Barbie's friend Midge, Barbie's sister Skipper and *her* buddy Skooter, as well as Skipper's boyfriend Ricky.

During the mid-1960s, at the peak of the "mod" fashion frenzy, plain-looking Midge lost out to some new British friends who sported the short, psychedelic, see-through threads popularized on Carnaby Street. Francie and Casey were the first; then came Twiggy, based on the slender – nearly invisible – fashion model of the day. (The real Twiggy has recently resurfaced in the entertainment field.) As if Barbie's Dream House (with pool) weren't crowded enough, she and Skipper then acquired twin siblings named Tutti and Todd.

By this time, a girl could make a career of playing with Barbie and her belongings. Mattel had licensed a lot of trappings for the original Material Girl, including a sports car with mag wheels and a licensed hot rod for Ken, both from the Irwin Company. A. J. Frank Company was

ABOVE: **During the mid-1960s, Barbie's Ballet Company, with Clara and Skipper, danced *The Nutcracker Suite*.**

LEFT: **Barbie and Ken's first Little Theatre, fit for a Tony Award production.**

RIGHT: **Barbie gets wheels. Her first sports car was this elegant convertible from the Irwin Company.**

TWIGGY
DRESS-UP KIT

You will love dressing TWIGGY in her beautiful clothes. Colorforms plastic sticks like magic. No scissors, no paste, never a muss.

a colorforms toy

twiggy
©1967 Minnow Co., Ltd. Printed in U.S.A.

LEFT: Colorforms came out with a dress-up kit for British high-fashion model Twiggy during the 1960s.

RIGHT: The Twiggy paper doll set, with dazzling fashions straight from Carnaby Street.

BOTTOM RIGHT: Teenage Tammy (right) and her Ideal family.

cranking out Barbie Bubble Bath, powder, and cologne. The Fashion Queen Barbie set came with three different wigs, and with the Color Magic Fashion Designer set you could customize Barbie's clothes with adhesive-backed glitter, flocking, and patterns – no sewing required.

Over the years, Mattel made many improvements to the original $3.00 Barbie herself. Her features were softened, her body became more flexible, her newly lashed eyes opened and closed. By 1970 Mattel was ready to introduce Living Barbie – an updated model that did everything but breathe. Eighteen years later, Barbie was the number one toy of the year, with her own biography, *Barbie: Her Life & Times*, published by Crown at $25.00 per copy. Not bad for a doll who had started life in a comic strip.

Of course, the Barbie phenomenon inspired a bevy of teen queens, including the Tressy doll from American Character, whose hair "grew" at the touch of a button. Tressy came with her own beauty salon, along with the requisite penthouse, clothes, and accessories. Dancing Dawn took this a step further, with her own late-1960s Disco, in which she twisted the night away with her boyfriend Kevin.

Ideal's contribution was Tammy, a teenaged doll with her own wardrobe and MGB sports car, who cruised across the TV screen in her "T" letter sweater every 15 minutes or so, waving to potential buyers. Then there was red-headed Crissy, a hair-growing doll who could be coiffed in such 1960s styles as the bubble cut and the flip. Valentine Dolls brought out its Twisteens line, with swivel-hipped action endorsed by that twistin' fool Chubby Checker.

LEFT: **Mattel's Baby First Step, who could walk *and* roller skate.**

ABOVE: **All of Mattel's Liddle Kiddles had big heads like Kleo Kola's.**

TOP, NEAR RIGHT: **Liddle Kiddle Sizzly Friddle and her barbecue set (1967).**

TOP, FAR RIGHT: **Cookie Sweet Treat Kiddle Chocolate Claire in her rather psychedelic pad.**

RIGHT: **The fetching Kiddle Kologne dolls bore out Mattel's premise that small was beautiful.**

ABOVE: **Mattel's Swingy doll did her own version of the Locomotion.**

RIGHT: **Mattel's Chatty Cathy had a bigger vocabulary than some second-graders.**

CENTER RIGHT: **Wigs were big in the 1960s, as attested to by this one-size-fits-all Character Wig kit.**

FAR RIGHT: **Ideal used real twins to publicize its Toni home-permanent doll, based on the hair-care manufacturer's campaign, "Which Twin Has the Toni?"**

ABOVE: **Hi Dottie was another loquacious doll from Mattel. Here, she talks on the phone to TV's Melissa Gilbert in 1972.**

But what had become of the baby dolls in all this discomania? Not surprisingly, Mattel kept this base covered too. ("You Can Tell It's Mattel – It's Swell!") There was Cheerful Tearful, another waterworks doll; Baby First Step, who could also (precociously) roller skate; Baby Secret, who talked into your ear; and a fetching line of minidolls called Liddle Kiddles, all under four inches tall, with big heads on tiny bodies that bent into various poses. Each had combable hair and changeable clothes.

Mattel also updated a popular talking doll named Chatty Cathy into the Charmin' Chatty of the late 1960s. This homely little-girl doll sported granny glasses, a sailor suit, and knee socks. She came with a supply of record discs that you inserted to keep the conversation going.

Not to be outdone, Kenner introduced Baby Alive, the best-selling doll of 1973. This doll did so many things you could have taken it home from the hospital nursery by mistake. Baby Alive moved her mouth when she ate or drank from her bottle. After you took the spoon out of her mouth, it looked like she was chewing. Bubbles appeared in the bottle when she drank. And that was only the beginning. The responsibility of owning this doll was awesome.

Merry Manufacturing wasn't idle during the 1960s, either. They continued making their high-fashion paper dolls, adding storybooks about them and vinyl "Rub 'n' Stay" clothes that could be interchanged. And should you get tired of primping and preening all those teenage dolls, you could go to work on yourself with the Miss Merry cosmetics sets – Beauty Sleep, Play Bath, and Model's Make-up. They, too, were "just like Mom's." It was, indeed, a small world.

ABOVE: **Three descendants of the original Davy Crockett gather for a publicity shot at the height of the Crockett craze.**

RIGHT: **Still more Crockett descendants appeared with host Garry Moore (center) on the popular TV show "I've Got a Secret" in 1955.**

FAR RIGHT: **Marx's Davy Crockett at the Alamo set had everything but a happy ending to the story.**

TOP RIGHT: **Crockett fever kept a lot of heads warm in 1955.**

The double whammy of Disney and television produced the first megacraze of the baby boom years: Davy Crockett. It was a black day for the raccoons of America when Disney aired the first of its three hour-long episodes on that rugged frontiersman at the end of 1954. (By then the "Disneyland" weekly series was a year old.) The demand for Davy Crockett frontier toys, weapons, and coonskin caps was instant and overwhelming. Within the year, more than 200 Davy Crockett items were on the market (including some not licensed by Disney, which couldn't copyright the Crockett name).

Daisy Manufacturing Company updated its popular air-rifle line to include a Davy Crockett rifle, canteen, and powder horn. The unquenchable Louis Marx turned out a 100-piece Davy Crockett at the Alamo set, including a metal fort with movable gates and fighting platforms, 30 frontiersmen plus Crockett himself, 30 Mexican soldiers, on foot and on horseback, and the many accessories that made Marx's playsets so popular. This set included a well, an andiron, a hitching post, and a water pump. Sears couldn't keep it in stock.

The 1955 *Toy Yearbook* featured the official Walt Disney Davy Crockett outfit, coonskin cap and all, plus a Walt Disney Frontierland Logs set that

looked suspiciously like that durable favorite, Lincoln Logs. The fad also spawned a host of lunchboxes, rubber Bowie knives, Hubley-style flintlocks and Derringers, comic books, archery sets, and 17 different recordings of the famous theme song "Davy, D-a-a-a-vy Crockett/King of the wild frontier!"

But within a year, Crockett fever had run its course, and boys were looking to other frontiersmen for inspiration. TV was happy to oblige. The 1950s and early 1960s were awash in popular Western series and characters, many of whom could also be seen at the movies. The 1950s were dominated by Hopalong Cassidy, Roy Rogers, the Lone Ranger, Gene Autry, the Cisco Kid, and Zorro.

Although Roy Rogers made his last Western movie in 1951, his palomino horse, Trigger, was still being billed as "the Smartest Horse in the Movies" in the mid-1950s, when every other kid in the country had something emblazoned with the Roy Rogers logo. Hubley offered a well-made cap pistol with a pearl-handled grip. Marx had two Roy Rogers playsets, Mineral City and the Double R Bar Ranch Rodeo, as well as the Roy Rogers' Fix-It Stagecoach, a great toy that included a tool kit for changing wheels, two grey horses in vinyl harness, and a driver with a whip and rifle. Other rolling stock included Marx's "official" Hauler and Van Trailer (for lugging around Trigger and Trigger Jr., plus Nellybelle the jeep). The King of the Cowboys also graced a horseshoe game, a walkie-

ABOVE: Cowboy star Bill Boyd appeared on the "authentic" Hopalong Cassidy outfit.

ABOVE RIGHT: In a colorful Zorro costume, "complete with mask," your own mother wouldn't know you.

RIGHT: The Lone Ranger's faithful mount was immortalized as a rocking horse.

FAR RIGHT: The masked man himself comes to the rodeo at Madison Square Garden in 1951.

talkie, a Ranch Lantern with a flashlight bulb, and a sand pail and shovel set, handy when the trail led to the beach or the sandbox.

Hopalong Cassidy ("Hoppy" for short) had been a popular Western movie character since the 1930s, but the black-suited cowboy, played by William Boyd, really came into his own after his 1948 television debut. Suddenly, the toymakers were there with Hopalong Cassidy guns and holsters, costumes, shooting galleries, tin wind-ups, dart boards, and a host of other licensed playthings. Gene Autry, who had reached the small screen a year earlier, also had a loyal following. Kenton made Gene Autry sidearms for their popular cap pistol line, Emenee produced a four-string guitar, there were ten-gallon hats aplenty, and others hopped onto the Autry buckboard too.

Few Western heroes could match the mysterious Lone Ranger in his black mask, thundering to the rescue on his beautiful horse, Silver, his Indian friend Tonto trailing doggedly in his wake. These two hit the trail together in 1933, on children's radio shows that aired for 15 minutes a day with various adventure series like "Tom Mix" and "Jack Armstrong, the All-American Boy." Even better than hearing the Lone Ranger was seeing him, which you could do in comic strips, comic books, the movies, and on TV from 1948 on. By that time, Kilgore had been turning out Lone Ranger six-shooters for years and other toy licensees were quick to ask, "Who *was* that masked man?" The rest, as they say, is history.

The Old Southwest was represented by the dashing Cisco Kid and his pudgy sidekick, Pancho, and Zorro, who went around making *Z*s on bad guys with his trademark whip. Both these heroes were big with the ladies on their TV shows, but like other members of the genre, Cisco and Zorro looked more romantic riding into the sunset than settling down in a little adobe house on the prairie. Zorro appeared in the 1959 Sears catalog as an eight-inch molded-plastic figure who foreshadowed the innumerable "action figures" of the decade to come. With him were Roy Rogers, Marshal Matt Dillon of "Gunsmoke," Jim Hardie of "Wells Fargo," Dan Troop of "Lawman," and Paladin of "Have Gun, Will Travel."

SHARE THE EXCITING ADVENTURES OF MARSHAL *Matt Dillon* IN

GUNSMOKE

AN ACTION PACKED WESTERN GAME

It's a LOWELL game

LOWELL TOY MFG. CORP., LONG ISLAND CITY, N. Y.

ABOVE: **Lowell's "Gunsmoke" board game, based on the popular Western TV series.**

RIGHT: **An ad for Daisy's Red Ryder carbine.**

LEFT: **Parker Brothers' "Have Gun Will Travel" game.**

ANNOUNCING
The Sensational New Daisy
1000-SHOT
RED RYDER
LICENSED BY STEPHEN SLESINGER, INC., NEW YORK
CARBINE
Western CARBINE RING
For SADDLE: TO HOLD CARBINE ON SADDLE
For HOME: TO HANG CARBINE ON WALL
FRED HARMAN
MY NEW LIGHTNING-LOADER REPEATER HAS A HEAP'O NEW FEATURES- LOOK 'EM OVER!
RED RYDER, America's favorite cowboy, is drawn by Fred Harman, nationally-famous Western Cowboy-Artist. Red Ryder rides in the daily, Sunday comic sections of hundreds of NEA-served newspapers. He's 6 feet of red-headed trigger lightning. Courageous. True-blue. Friend of the poor. Foe of the wicked. Watch for him—and Little Beaver—in your newspaper.
CARBINE RING . . . the only air rifle in the world with genuine Western Style Carbine Ring anchored in jacket!
16-INCH LEATHER SADDLE THONG knotted to Carbine Ring.
1000-SHOT . . . The first 1000-shot repeating Carbine in air rifle history!
GOLDEN BANDS . . . the first and only Daisy with Golden Bands . . . on muzzle and hand-hold . . . symbolizing "The Golden West!"
RED RYDER BRANDED STOCK . . . Red Ryder's official signature, picture and horse "Thunder" are all branded into Carbine Stock!
LIGHTNING-LOADER . . . the only 1000-Shot Daisy with Lightning Loader Invention!
LONGER BARREL . . . Red Ryder Carbine barrel is 3 in. longer than Daisy's original 500-shot Lightning-Loader Carbine!
FULL-LENGTH HAND-HOLD
COCKING-LEVER
FINISH
IT'S A DAISY
IT'S REALLY YOURS for only $2.95
out of the Golden West...
RYDER brings YOU this beautiful
GOLDEN-BANDED DAISY
Daisy's brand-new, big, 1000-Shot RED RYDER CARBINE . . . Golden Bands . . . the gun with the Carbine RING . . . the RYDER'S name, picture, and horse "Thunder" branded into the NEW gun YOU'VE SIMPLY GOT TO GET! Picture yourself riding this husky RED RYDER CARBINE lashed to your saddle thru Carbine RING . . . loading her up with 1000 shot in just 20 . . . drawing a bead through the Adjustable DOUBLE-NOTCH REAR . . . "BANG! BANG! BANG!" as fast as you can work the CARBINE . . . up to ONE THOUSAND SHOTS without once re-loading! What a gun! A Carbine . . . a REAL Western Carbine. The kind Western Movies and on the range. Fred Harman (famous cowboy- the exciting RED RYDER comic strip) used to fork a bronc 'way out West himself—and Fred helped Daisy design this RED RYDER CARBINE. So, it looks real. It feels real. And Carbine BARK! How happy you'll be with this beautiful RED RYDER CARBINE! Dash down now to your nearest goods or department store—and BUY IT! Honest-to-Goodness! SHOT RED RYDER CARBINE costs you only $2.95! If your there's no Daisy Dealer near you) send the $2.95 direct your RED RYDER CARBINE to you POSTPAID!
The Popular
500 SHOT LIGHTNING-LOADER CARBINE
This is Daisy's original 500-shot Carbine, featuring Lightning-Loader Invention and Adjustable DOUBLE-NOTCH REAR SIGHT. If you can't afford the brand-new feature-crammed RED RYDER 1000-SHOT CARBINE at $2.95—then get THIS 500-SHOT beauty for $2.50 at Dealers or direct. (Duty added in Canada).
Just out! Pictures of all Daisys from $1 to $5. Write!
CATALOG
USE DAISY BULLS EYE SHOT
BIG JUMBO TUBE 5¢
Buy genuine Daisy-made "CHROME-SHEEN" steel Bulls Eye Shot—for accurate shooting in Daisy and King Air Rifles. It's BEST. At your Dealers.
DAISY AIR RIFLES
LITTLE BEAVER
RED RYDER'S

Helping all these heroes keep law and order on the frontier required an arsenal, and Mattel did its part with the Shootin' Shell Fanner 50, which not only fired caps, but also ejected "shells." The regular model Fanner 50 came with a low-cut holster that enabled you to make the quickest draw on the block. Mattel's Winchester saddle gun (with bandolier) also fired caps and ejected shells, with a repeating feature that shot off multiple rounds. Then there was the Buckle Gun – a weapon like none ever seen in the West. A tiny Derringer in your belt buckle could be fired by sticking out your stomach, even if you were hog-tied. Fortunately, Mattel also offered a full line of ammunition: Greenie Stik-M-Caps, Shootin' Shell cartridges, and bullet noses.

Hubley had been the leader in cast-iron toys and cap pistols before World War II, when it switched over to die-cast zinc alloys – lighter, and cheaper to ship. Its last classic cast-iron toy was the Texan revolver – over nine inches long – which was made with the customary Hubley quality and attention to detail. It was so heavy that smaller kids had to pick it up with both hands. During the 1950s, Hubley's Ric-O-Shay gun included a speaker that produced a loud, whiny ricochet sound every time you fired it. This toy was neck-and-neck with Daisy's No. 960 Noisemaker for sheer volume. The Daisy Pump Gun was advertised as "the king of all BB guns." BB guns caused high parental anxiety, but kids had been demanding them since 1888, when 86,000 were sold.

W. J. Murphy offered a realistic-looking line of Tru-Blu handguns with wooden grips that you could notch yourself (pocketknife included). The Pinto gun, from Nichols Industries, was a Derringer with a flip-out cylinder. It fired one cap cartridge at a time. The Bop-A-Bear set came with a suction-cup dart-shooting rifle and a big battery-powered plastic bear that rolled forward until you zapped it with a dart. Then it turned around and growled at you.

By 1953, when he issued his long-running Fort Apache Playset, Louis Marx had been making toys for more than 30 years. Born in 1896 to German immigrant parents, he got his start with the firm of Ferdinand Strauss, a major early-1900s toymaker. When Strauss went bankrupt, Marx and his brother David bought the defunct company's dies and molds and went into business as the Marx Company, which flourished. Louis Marx was a millionaire by the time he was 25. He offered value for money and produced a bewildering variety of toys, especially metal litho and elaborate playsets prized by both kids and collectors. By 1974 the durable Fort Apache Playset had a metal headquarters building, 41 cavalry figures, 15 Indians, a campfire, scaling ladders for the stockade fence, cordwood, chopping block, cookstand, blockhouses, a well, a tepee, a totem pole, and horses – all for $8.49.

Little kids rode the range on untippable rocking horses made of plastic, suspended by springs from a metal frame. Cowboy hats, vests, chaps, boots, and other regalia came in all sizes – cowgirls weren't excluded – and Mattel provided a Cowboy Ge-tar and Music Box that cranked out "Red River Valley" when you turned the handle.

When the TV series "Bonanza" took off, Marx was there with a detailed Johnny West Adventure Series, including a 31-piece Chief Cherokee set, buckboard, covered wagon, and horses Pancho, Thunderbolt, Buckskin, Comanche, and Stormcloud. American Character made a set of Bonanza Action Men, including Ben, Little Joe, and Hoss Cartwright in

LEFT: **War whoops scare off marauding settlers from the next block.**

RIGHT: **A man can't be too careful in this part of town.**

BELOW: **A young cowpoke takes a well-earned rest.**

93

jointed plastic, with accessories like the Four-In-One Chuckwagon. "Bonanza" was at least as popular in the U.K. as it was in the U.S.

The "Wagon Train" series inspired a toy pistol, and Wyatt Earp rated a long-barrelled Buntline Special 50-cap repeater and a miniature Dodge City, complete with the Silver Dollar music hall with swinging doors.

Then, too, there were crime shows, such as "Dragnet," "Martin Kane, Private Eye," "Peter Gunn," "The Untouchables," and "Highway Patrol." Crime shows and comic strips featuring hard-boiled detectives such as Dick Tracy were fertile ground for shoot-'em-up fantasies.

Hawk-faced Dick Tracy had been around since the 1930s, when he had his own radio show and comic strip, peopled by exotic villains and chain-smoking colleagues. Marx offered a metal litho Dick Tracy Police Station with car during the 1950s. Ideal had a Dick Tracy Copmobile, battery-operated by remote control. The Dick Tracy Target Game from American Character featured a Silent Ray Gun that "shot through glass" with a flashlight beam.

Some cow ponies can do everything but talk...

Blaze, here, is the exception. He does talk. Says eleven different things, even snorts and whinnies. Out there alone on the moonlit prairie, a cowpoke can get mighty lonely. So it's good to have a horse to talk to. But Blaze does more. His legs move as he gallops, trots, and rears. He is just one of the intriguing products of Mattel Toymakers.

Your child may see one of these toys on our television programs. If he should ask for that toy, you can be confident of thoughtful originality and uncompromising quality. That quality is important to children ... and to us. Because ours is a most rewarding business. We make children happy.

MATTEL, INC. TOYMAKERS

(reverse), please write to Mattel, Inc.— P. O. Box 521, Dept. AD, Hawthorne, California

94

FAR LEFT: **Mattel's active pinto cow pony, Blaze, even talked.**

ABOVE: **Chester Gould's Dick Tracy in a "Crime Does Not Pay Club" puzzle.**

LEFT: **Water pistols helped make-believe detectives get their man.**

ABOVE RIGHT: **A toy copy of the machine gun toted by "federal agents" in "The Untouchables" TV series.**

TOP RIGHT: **Good-looking Robert Stack starred in "The Untouchables" as crimebuster Elliot Ness.**

The popular "Dragnet" series, with stone-faced Jack Webb as Sergeant Joe Friday, was grittily realistic. Webb directed the series too, and the stories were based on real criminal cases in the files of the Los Angeles Police Department. ("Only the names have been changed to protect the innocent," intoned the voice-over prologue.) Friday's deadpan instruction to overexcited witnesses – "Just the facts, ma'am, just the facts" – became a catch phrase of the times, and the show inspired a series of true-to-life police weapons for would-be crimebusters.

Another exciting crime show was "The Untouchables," which starred Robert Stack as righteous Elliot Ness in pursuit of Prohibition-era gangsters. The series began late in 1959 and ran for four years. Louis Marx produced an "Untouchables" Playset that included Al Capone and fellow gangsters, plainclothes detectives, policemen, machine guns, a corpse, a warehouse, two 1920s cars, even a tank for brewing bathtub gin – all correct to the last exciting detail.

95

"77 Sunset Strip" didn't take itself too seriously as a detective show. Its best-remembered character was a hair-combing car attendant named Kookie, who inspired a popular song. "Highway Patrol," with Broderick Crawford, had everyone saying "Ten-four!" into his imaginary squad-car radio. Strombecker produced a Hiway Patrol road-race set with two intersections that promised high-speed collisions between the police car, with its flashing red lights and siren, and a hot rod cruising for trouble.

World War II, the Korean conflict, and Vietnam all spawned war toys and military shows for a new generation. Traditional military toys like tin and lead soldiers and knights in armor on their armored steeds remained popular, with some changes in material and designs.

Toy historian Richard O'Brien reports that metal soldiers (probably imported from England) were sold in America as early as 1777. The *Tory Royal Gazette* advertised them as Christmas presents "for the Young Folks who have an affection for the Art Military, consisting of Horse, Foot and Dragoons. Cast in metal, in beautiful uniforms."

ABOVE: **Toy Tommy guns added realism to guerrilla activities in the neighborhood.**

TOP RIGHT: **Trainer rifles were carried on woodlot patrols.**

RIGHT: **In 1962 Emenee produced an electronic rifle range whose target lit up when hit by "bullets of light" from rifles operated on transistor batteries.**

New York's McLoughlin Brothers produced paper soldiers mounted on cardboard for more than 80 years, from 1857. Printed in striking colors, the six-inch-tall British set consisted of Black Watch Highlanders, Infantry of the Line, and a Guards Band. About 1910 McLoughlin Brothers began to distribute toy soldiers from solid-lead castings.

Britains Soldiers had been manufacturing lead soldiers in the U.K. for well over a century. C. W. Beiser copied their designs for the U.S. market when he founded American Soldier in New York in 1898. Beiser's hollow-cast lead soldiers were usually painted in the standard way; some were made in gold, or black and gold.

Milton Bradley entered the fray in 1910 with his colorful cardboard Soldiers on Parade set. Bright red and blue were favored for uniforms, even if they had little to do with the armies of the day. Bright colors brought increased sales, not only to boys, but to their dads as well.

Metal soldiers were popular playthings until World War II, when defense needs pre-empted the supply of lead and other metals. Toy-makers soldiered on with cardboard, wood, or composition figures and accessories, including B-29s, PT boats, jeeps, submarines, tanks, and trucks. Molded Products resorted to a mix of wood flour, starch, whiting, and water for its miniature armies. Even though they melted in the rain, toy-hungry boys made them big sellers. Hubley's authentic cast-iron Army .45 was also popular.

The postwar years brought many new plastics and rubberlike compounds that were a boon to toy manufacturers. Metal litho remained popular, as in Marx's highly detailed Rex Mars Tank, which doubled as a space toy. (Marx always got a lot of mileage from his products.) Unique offered a tin litho machine gun with a shoulder strap, and Hubley made U.S. Army Air Corps planes like the Seversky P-35. The newer materials were represented by the detailed plastic U.S. Combat Patrol Set from Halco and Marx's Army Training Center Set – 145 (count 'em) pieces for $5.98. That's more toys than some kids had through their whole child-hoods. Marx also offered The Big Parade – a battery-powered military band that marched in cadence.

Boyish enthusiasm for these militant toys was fanned by popular TV shows like "Combat," "Rat Patrol," and "Convoy." There was a Tommy gun – Thompson submachine gun – to suit every need that could arise on a back yard or woodlot patrol. One version fired over 840 shots per minute, accompanied by electric sparks. Mattel's metal-and-plastic Tommy Burp Gun – advertised on the new "Mickey Mouse Club" show at a cost equal to the company's net worth at the time – turned out not to be a shot in the dark. The Burp Gun zoomed to the pinnacle of the sales charts with a noisy roar – and a barrel that smoked.

Topper really went over the top with its Johnny Seven One Man Army Gun. This portable Defense Department had no fewer than seven features, including grenade and anti-tank rocket launchers, armor-piercing and anti-bunker missiles, and a detachable automatic cap pistol. With this weapon and Tudor Metal's olive-drab walkie talkie (with emergency button), you could safely go anywhere in the neighborhood.

Remco made an imposing fleet of plastic battleships, including the three-foot-long Fighting Lady, available at Sears for $8.88. Its gun rotated, fired, and ejected shells. It also launched a plane and fired depth charges. The Barracuda Submarine, according to Remco's 1964 catalog,

TOP LEFT: **Britain's Soldiers' 11th Hussars – Prince Albert's Own – dismounted.**

LEFT: **Britain's metal soldiers of World War I.**

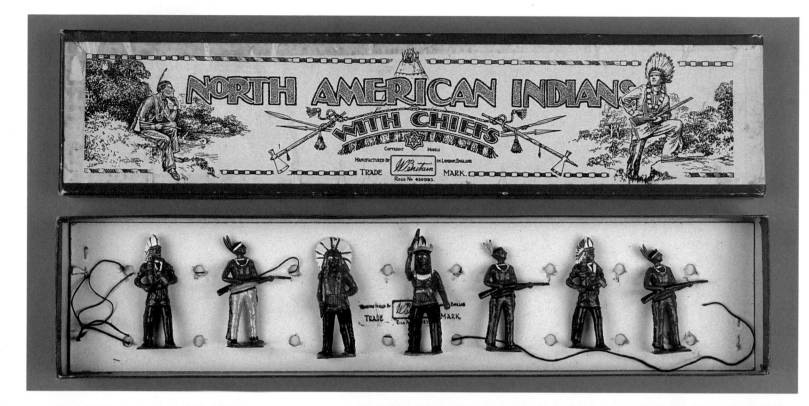

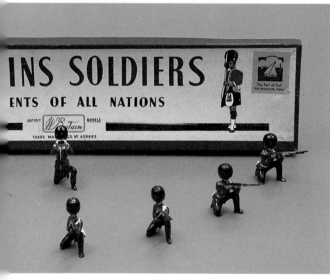

ABOVE: **Britain's Coldstream Guards, from the Regiments of All Nations series.**

TOP: **Britain's colorful North American Indians set was an innovation for the venerable U.K. firm long known for its lead soldiers.**

RIGHT: **World War I vehicles, ordnance, and soldiers faithfully reproduced in the Britain's Soldiers tradition.**

Desert treasure holds
clues to mystery . .
can he find it?

ADVENTURE
TEAM VEHICLE

Mad gorilla ahead
. . does he get away?

Trapped by avalanche
. . will he escape?

G. I. Joe 3-in-1 Super Adventure Set

Take G. I. Joe into the seething jungle,
desert heat and cold Arctic dangers

*Sold only
at Sears*

$12⁴⁹ without G. I. Joe,
boots, batteries

All the accessories needed to take G.I. Joe on three exciting adventures. He travels to the desert in his
ATV car. Car floats in water or rolls on land, has working winch. Other desert equipment includes helmet,
mummy and case, shovel, pick, net. Suit not included. Brave jungle dangers and pigmy gorilla in battery-
powered boat, tent. Or he meets Arctic hazards in ski outfit (pants, hooded parka, gloves). Husky dog with
harness pulls sled. Plastic. Uses 1 "C" battery, order pkg. below.
79 C 59135C—Shipping weight 6 pounds...Set $12.49
49 C 8411—Alkaline "C" Batteries. Pkg. of 4. Wt. 8 oz.....................................Pkg. 2.49

G. I. Joe Footlocker

$3⁹⁹

G.I. Joe's ready for
any inspection.
Wooden locker has
removable tray . .
holds plenty of Joe's
equipment. Rope
handles. 13½x6½x
4¾ in. high. Shipping
weight 2 pounds.
49 C 59081 . . . . $3.99

The action starts here . .
G. I. Joe Adventure
Team Headquarters

$13⁹⁹ without
batteries

3-room "building" has working blink-
er, telegraph key, telescoping tower.
Map, storage rooms with accessories.
Vinyl; folds into case. 34x11x30 in.
high. 2 "D" batteries, order below.
79 C 59176C—Wt. 4 lbs. . . . Set $13.99

Alkaline "D" Batteries. Pkg. of 4.
49 C 8412—Wt. 1 lb. . . . . . . Pkg. $3.29

FAR LEFT: **G.I. Joe's adventures took him to desert, jungle, and Arctic terrains, but he was equipped for anything.**

LEFT: **Hasbro's original G.I. Joe action figure, armed to the teeth, came out in 1964.**

ABOVE: **G.I. Joe's U.S. Army tank was authentic to the last rivet.**

BELOW: **With enough G.I. Joe accessories, you could start your own war.**

had a "transparent deck and motorized twin propellers. Nuclear reactor flashes red, warning chime rings. Missiles fire automatically, torpedos fire mechanically." Remco also offered a variety of army toys, including a remote control tank, a radar rocket cannon, and a radio station.

During the 1960s, Barclay had the metal-miniature field covered with personnel from the various services, plus cowboys, Indians, and medieval knights. The Union City, New Jersey, manufacturer also offered small tanks, cannon, and three-piece equipment sets at less than a dollar each. Mattel produced several toys related to the Vietnam War, including camouflage outfits and the M-16 Marauder Semiautomatic Rifle. But the surprise war toy of the decade was Hasbro's G.I. Joe action figure, complete with battle-scarred cheek and "lifelike hair."

G.I. Joe, 11 inches tall, could be manipulated into just about any combat position: he was jointed at the neck, shoulders, arms, waist, and legs. Armed with rifle, pistol, and/or machine gun, Joe appeared in 1964 complete with combat boots, dog tags, and olive-drab soldier's uniform. You could also get him as an Action Sailor, an Action Marine, and an Air Force Action Pilot. His gear included pup tents, weapons, scuba-diving equipment, seabags, helmets, and enough other stuff to make Mattel's civilian Ken doll pale with envy. (But G.I. Joe was never, *ever* called a doll. He was a "moveable soldier.")

The burgeoning civil rights movement inspired a black G.I. Joe in 1965, followed by Hasbro's Soldiers of the World line. You could get a head start on World War III with accurately equipped British Commandos, Australian Jungle Fighters, French Resistance Fighters, Japanese, German, and Soviet soldiers. Jeeps and helicopters abounded, and in 1966, G.I. Joe joined the race into space with a Space Capsule set that could be retrieved after splashdown in the bathtub. But by 1966, the

Vietnam War was becoming so thorny an issue that G.I. Joe as a Green Beret aroused more protests than sales. Hasbro quickly shifted the toy's emphasis, creating an Adventure Team that went around the world being macho, but not necessarily military.

Meanwhile, Marx had introduced a flexible paratrooper named Stony who was – oddly enough – exactly Joe's size. But antiwar sentiment and the growing popularity of escapist spy shows and their toy offspring had ushered in a new craze by the mid-1960s.

It started with Ian Fleming's James Bond, better known in British Military Intelligence circles as Agent 007. Bond's exotic cars, weapons, women, and enemies appeared to good advantage in the 1962 movie *Dr. No*, starring Sean Connery as 007, closely followed by *Thunderball* and *Goldfinger*. Gilbert got into the intelligence game with a host of 3¼-inch plastic Bond figures, including Dr. No, Largo, "M," Miss Moneypenny, Oddjob, and Goldfinger. Bond and the sinister Oddjob, with his blade-rimmed killer hat, also appeared as 11-inch action figures. Oddjob's package copy was inspired: "Throws Deadly Derby! Delivers Swift Karate Blow!" The hefty villain's arms were spring operated, the right arm hurling the hat and the left chopping downward "like an axe."

"The Man from U.N.C.L.E." TV series was a first cousin to Bond. It appeared in 1964 and ran for four years, to the joy of toymakers like Aurora Plastics, which added the characters to its model-kit line. Gilbert produced 11-inch replicas of the show's stars, including Illya Kuryakin,

played by handsome, blond David McCallum. Based loosely on G.I. Joe, Illya was less mobile, but he sported the requisite secret-agent black turtleneck and pants and fired caps from his die-cast metal pistol.

Dream cars like AMT's Piranha were an exciting feature of espionage activities. Imported dream cars included the James Bond Aston-Martin from Mettoy Playcraft Ltd. under their Corgi brand name. Long known for its finely made car miniatures, the U.K. firm entered the novelty car field in the mid-1960s with licenses to manufacture cars like the Bond Aston-Martin, which had a flip-up bulletproof shield and an emergency ejection seat. Corgi also produced a Man from U.N.C.L.E. sedan with a roof-top siren. When you pressed it, little Napoleon Solos and Illya Kuryakins popped out of their seats to fire pistols.

Gimmickry was rampant, in the best secret-service tradition. Eldon produced a line of spy squirt toys in the form of cameras, pens, knives, and so forth. Marx had an U.N.C.L.E. shooting cane, and Mattel offered the Agent Zero M Movie-Shot Camera. "The Man from U.N.C.L.E." and its spinoff, "The Girl from U.N.C.L.E.," also inspired a Jump Suit Set, a Target Set, and an aptly named Arsenal set. It consisted of a cap-firing Tommy gun and pistol, a spring-loaded bazooka, shells, a bipod, a sight, and a rifle butt for converting the pistol into a long-range weapon.

By the late 1960s, however, all the soldier and spy toys were looking nervously over their shoulders at a new development: superheroes, from Batman to space men. The race to the moon was on.

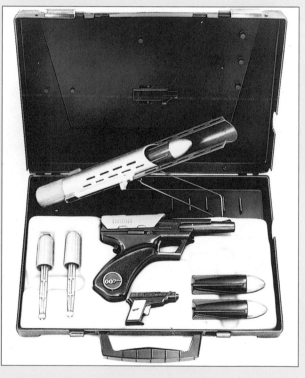

TOP LEFT: **A. C. Gilbert's James Bond, 007, and Oddjob vinyl action puppets.**

LEFT: **Ten figures from the 007 movie thrillers, including the sinister Dr. No.**

ABOVE: **The portable 007 arsenal included a missile launcher.**

TOP CENTER: **Corgi's action-adventure vehicles, including Bond's Aston Martin DB.5.**

5. TO THE MOON!

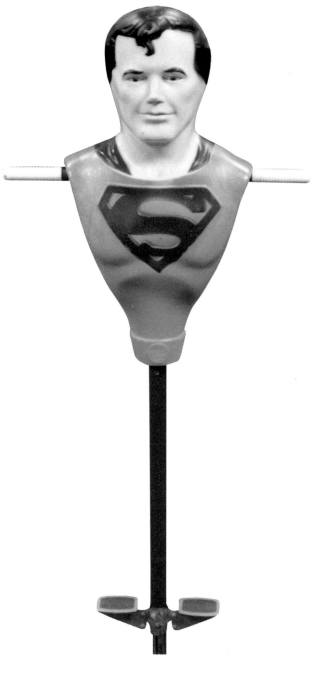

Both science and science fiction had been fascinating kids at least since Jules Verne, but sometimes the line between the two got pretty blurry. Space-age toys had been around for decades, but they got a new impetus in 1957, when the Soviet Union launched its *Sputnik* satellite. The following year, the United States sent its first satellite into orbit, and NASA had high visibility throughout the 1960s with its program for putting a man on the moon before the decade was out. Old comic-strip heroes like Buck Rogers, Captain Video, Flash Gordon, and Captain Midnight were dusted off and put into TV series along with a host of new heroes – super and otherwise – who represented the triumph of technology, not to mention imagination.

Children's-hour adventure shows on 1930s radio had included "Buck Rogers," "Captain Midnight," and "Superman," each with an avid following. All of them offered premiums in the form of small toys that appeared in sponsors' cereal boxes or could be sent away for at a dime or less. The Buck Rogers comic-strip resulted in a line of metal space pistols from Daisy and a set of Buck Rogers spacecraft from Tootsietoy, including the Flash-Blast Attack Ship and Venus Duo-Destroyer, which were good sellers even in Depression days. Louis Marx produced a line of tin wind-ups, including the red-and-green Buck Rogers Police Patrol rocket.

TOP LEFT: **Buck Rogers and Flash Gordon tin wind-up rockets from Marx.**

TOP CENTER: **George Reeves takes off as Superman in the popular TV series.**

LEFT: **Tootsietoy's Buck Rogers rocket ships and Captain Marvel "Lightning" race cars from Automatic Toy.**

LEFT: **A superhero didn't leave home without his Superman cape and space gun.**

ABOVE: **A Superman pogo stick gave you the jump on the competition.**

Superman starred in the first issue of *Action Comics* in 1938, and a year later, Ideal was making the man from Krypton in jointed wood and composition, painted (of course) blue and red. By the late 1950s, Superman had his own battery-operated tank, made by Linemar (a Marx subsidiary based in Japan) and a host of costumes and figures popularized by his long-running TV series, which began in 1952.

Lingering unease about some of the new technology was reflected in the mythic origins of many scientific sci-fi toys. Spiderman got his mysterious powers as the result of being bitten by a radioactive spider affected during an experiment. Spiderman, like the Incredible Hulk after him, had started life in a comic book. When the Hulk reached the TV screen, he was popping buttons off size 18½ extra-large shirts when he flew into a rage and throwing bears the length of a football field – all as a result of accidental "cobalt bomb radiation." In his former mild-mannered guise as a research scientist, he'd never tossed bears around or turned green.

"Batman," based on a long-running comic-book character, was a spoof that succeeded beyond its creators' wildest dreams when it came to TV in 1966. The campy Caped Crusader and his sidekick, Robin, seized the attention of the whole country and opened the merchandising floodgates. Toys, costumes, games, gimmicks – even peanut butter –

appeared under the Batman aegis to the tune of $150 million in the show's first year alone. Corgi made a Batmobile, which was imported from the U.K., and Transogram put out a Flying Batman figure ("He zooms, soars and loops through the air!") Holy Superhero – another trend!

Not to be outdone, Ideal had created an all-purpose superhero called Captain Action, an inch taller than the prototype action figure, G.I. Joe. Weather-beaten Captain Action came with the obligatory turtleneck *cum* insignia, pants and plastic boots, plus a lightning-shaped sword and a pistol that looked like a ray gun. Better yet, you could transform him into other heroes – Superman, Aquaman, Batman, and seven more – by changing not only his clothes, but his head! Soon Captain Action was joined by Action Boy, an interchangeable sidekick who could function as Robin, Superboy, or Aqua Lad. Wait, there's more. Ideal then created an inspired villain in the form of Dr. Evil, who came with truly menacing accessories like a hypodermic rifle and a false face that could be ripped off. All this plus a Secret Chamber and a Silver Streak car.

"Captain Video" was launched in 1949, from a "secret mountain head-quarters" on Planet Earth, whence he fought the forces of evil throughout the universe until 1957. Along the way, he inspired a host of toys – mostly premiums – ranging from the Rite-O-Lite flashlight to the inevitable Secret Seal Ring. The show's budget was ludicrously low, but kids had little critical faculty in those early days of television, so it didn't make any difference.

"Tom Corbett, Space Cadet" was reprised in Marx's Tom Corbett 25th-Century Space Academy of 1952, and Flash Gordon was represented by a futuristic water pistol and a Radio Repeater Click Pistol. Buck Rogers faced the 1950s with Norton-Honer's plastic Sonic Ray and Super Sonic Ray Guns. The "Fireball XL 5" show was big with British kids, who also took the made-in-America "Star Trek" series to their hearts. Trekkies on both sides of the Atlantic were suiting up in plastic space helmets and aiming ray guns at each other.

TOP LEFT: **Playcraft Ltd.'s Batmobile could fire three rockets and was equipped with a chain-slashing blade and "turbine jet exhaust."**

LEFT: **Adam West played the Caped Crusader on the campy "Batman" TV series.**

TOP: **Batmania swept the country in the 1960s as the lifesize Batmobile roared through the streets of television's Gotham City.**

ABOVE: **This cowboy strayed off the range into a Batman fantasy with the help of a pair of Batman blinkers.**

107

BELOW: **Milton Bradley's Captain Video puzzle.**

RIGHT: **The Space Cadets in a puzzle from 1952.**

TOP RIGHT: **Tom Corbett, Space Cadet, was among the first in the race to the moon. The puzzle is from the early 1950s.**

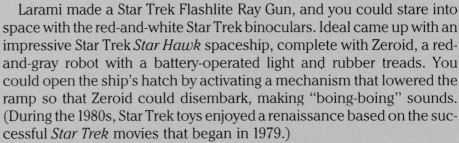

Larami made a Star Trek Flashlite Ray Gun, and you could stare into space with the red-and-white Star Trek binoculars. Ideal came up with an impressive Star Trek *Star Hawk* spaceship, complete with Zeroid, a red-and-gray robot with a battery-operated light and rubber treads. You could open the ship's hatch by activating a mechanism that lowered the ramp so that Zeroid could disembark, making "boing-boing" sounds. (During the 1980s, Star Trek toys enjoyed a renaissance based on the successful *Star Trek* movies that began in 1979.)

Wyandotte – best known for its metal cars and trucks – had produced a Rocket Racer spaceship in the mid-1930s, when both Buck Rogers and Flash Gordon were making converts to pulp novels like *Amazing Stories* and *Argosy*. By the late 1950s, Japanese manufacturers were making a

dent in the space-toy market with realistic Moon Rockets and Moon Space Ships (battery-operated), plus a friction-powered Two-Stage Earth Satellite. These appeared in the 1958 Sears Christmas catalog alongside Marx's Cape Canaveral Rocket Set with its 60-plus pieces.

When the 1960s arrived, space toys moved away from the fantastic towards greater realism – as interpreted by American toymakers. Robots were still popular, but more sophisticated than they'd been in the 1950s. In 1961 Robot Commando from Ideal turned right or left, responded to spoken commands, and fired rockets and missiles. The popular "Lost in Space" series spawned a foot-high plastic robot with a flashing light instead of a head. This metallic companion to the "Lost in Space" Robinson family was in the tradition of the great sci-fi films of the 1950s, including *The Day the Earth Stood Still* and *Forbidden Planet*, which featured helpful rather than menacing robots.

Ideal's mid-1950s 14-inch Robert the Robot, with plastic hand control and crank-operated voice mechanism, was updated in the 1960s to include a feature that fired missiles from his head. Mattel improved upon this concept with its Lost in Space Roto-Jet Gun, which not only fired missiles but also made an eerie shrieking sound.

Mr. Machine started walking off toy counters in 1960. He was a popular educational robot from Ideal, whose see-through plastic body revealed complex inner workings of nuts, bolts, and gears. Activated by a wind-up key in his back, and topped by a plastic hat, Mr. Machine could be taken apart and put back together. Ideal updated him in the late 1970s with a bellows-operated whistling feature and actions that included rolling forward on big plastic wheels, swinging his arms, opening and closing his mouth, and turning the gears inside. The new version couldn't be disassembled, but he did whistle "This Old Man" in tuneful style.

LEFT: The "Smokey Joe" Thunder Gun shot ping pong balls at aliens from outer space.

CENTER: Pointy-eared Mr. Spock of "Star Trek" became a cult figure for Trekkies around the world.

BELOW: Posable Star Trek figures *al fresco.*

RIGHT: Cragston's Mr. Atomic robot had an imposing array of lights and actions.

LEFT: **A youthful spaceman prepares to blast off in his Erector set rocket ship.**

LEFT: **Robert the Robot stops traffic at the 1954 New York Toy Fair.**

BELOW: **Squinting through his space helmet, an 8-year-old astronaut launches a satellite from his Ideal space truck.**

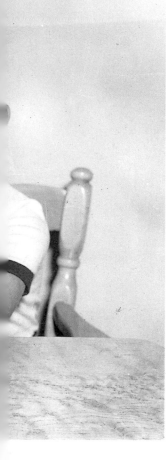

TOP LEFT: **Power play: the walking, talking Robert the Robot from Ideal.**

LEFT: **Shown at the 1956 Toy Fair in New York, "The Brain" was maneuvered by a mystifying "Z-Man" in a variety of pre-set patterns that included firing guided missiles.**

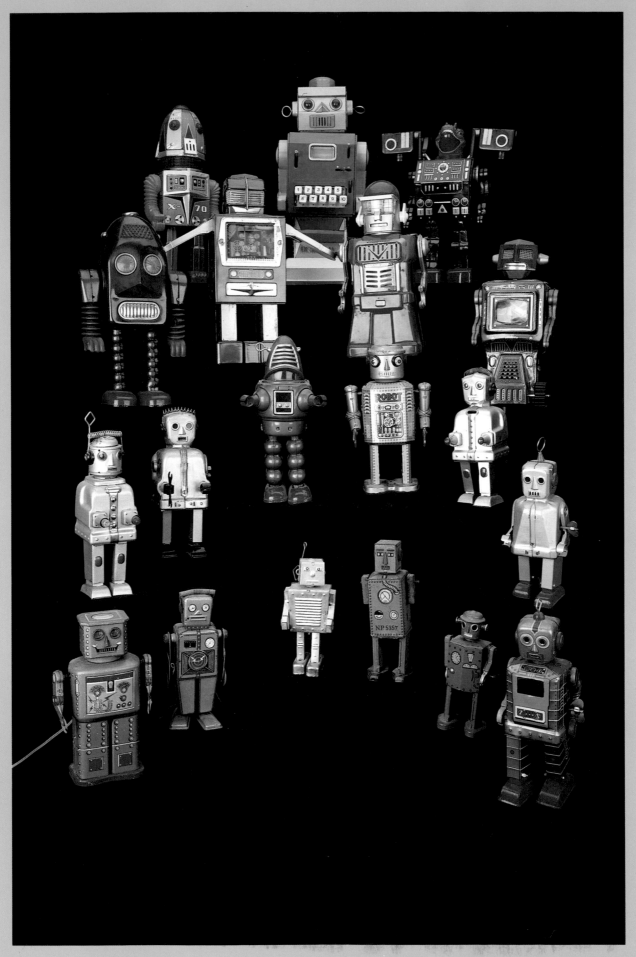

LEFT: **A collection of colorful robots from the 1940s-1960s.**

TOP: **Gilbert's Martian Magic Tricks set, 1965, was inspired by Ray Walston's title character in TV's "My Favorite Martian".**

ABOVE: **The intriguing Mr. Machine from Ideal.**

RIGHT: **Major Matt Mason makes a three-point landing.**

Turn dial to make toy move forward, in reverse, left, right, at random, or stop

Magic Dial Toys obey your command

Each $**4**⁷⁷ without batteries

Just turn the dial, and each of these 3 space toys lights up. Then they turn in whatever direction the arrow on the dial is pointing. You choose the direction. All plastic. Each uses 2 "C" batteries. Order package below.

1 Space Dog. 7¾x4¼x7 in.
49 N51063—Wt. 1 lb. 8 oz. $4.77
2 Space Saucer. 10x10¼x4½ in.
49 N51062—Wt. 1 lb. 8 oz. $4.77
3 Space Robot. 9½x7x9½ in.
49 N51064—Wt. 1 lb. 8 oz. $4.77
"C" Batteries. Package of 6.
49 N 8406—Wt. 12 oz. Pkg. $1.19

Giant 13-inch Robot

Walks backward, forward, and in a circle while his eyes flash.. you control him by remote control

$**7**⁹⁹
without batteries

This robot emits an eerie mechanical sound, and his eyes flash as he walks along, swinging his arms. You control his movements by flipping 2 switches on remote control attachment. Made of metal and plastic. A full 13 inches high. Uses 2 "D" batteries. Order package below. Buy it the easy way—order by phone.
49 N 5104—Shipping weight 2 pounds 12 ounces.........$7.99
49 N 8405—"D" Batteries. Package of 6. Wt. 1 lb. 8 oz. Pkg. 1.49

STAR TEAM

by Ideal

It's great to pretend you're walking on the moon

Space Helmet and Boots $**9**⁸⁸ set

Equipment Belt $**5**⁹⁹

Space Helmet and Boots. Space helmet of amber gold-color break-resistant plastic fits all sizes. Collar has finned louvers and vent for receiving "life-support" tube. Headphone nonoperative. Molded plastic air-cushioned boots have laces, adjust to fit. Large-lugged soles leave impressive footprints, and a low-pitched whistle accents each step. For ages 5 to 10 years.
79 N 53061C—Helmet and Boots. Shipping weight 5 pounds.........Set $9.88
79 N 53062C—Helmet only. Shipping weight 3 pounds.........4.88
Equipment Belt. Carries anti-gravity tool, signal communicator, "life-support system," and scanner scope. Plastic. Adjusts to fit waists up to 27 in.
49 N 53063—Equipment Belt. Shipping weight 1 pound 8 oz.........$5.99

Naughty Robot walks and twists like a dancer

$**2**⁹⁹
without batteries

This little guy twists his body as though he's really proud of himself. Light blinks on his chest as he struts along. Made of strong metal and plastic. 7 in. high. Uses 2 "AA" batteries. Order package below. Shpg. wt. 12 oz.
49 N 5103.........$2.99
"AA" Batteries. Package of 6.
49 N 8402—Shpg. wt. 6 oz. Pkg. 99c

PCBKM AEDSL Sears 47

LEFT: **Space toys from Sears' 1970 Christmas catalog.**

BELOW: **Aurora's daunting "Lost in Space" robot, with Slinky-like arms.**

RIGHT: **Two thumbs up for a NASA space doll shown at the 1961 American Rocket Society Exhibition.**

BELOW RIGHT: **The cast of CBS-TV's popular "Lost in Space" series.**

FAR RIGHT: **Estes Industries' Alpha Deluxe model rocket set.**

Ideal surpassed itself with robotic King Zor, which resembled some of the many hilarious monsters being created in all seriousness by Japanese moviemakers: fuzzy gigantic Mothra (a moth), reptilian Godzilla, and a rather shabby-looking version of King Kong that grappled with the others while a miniature Tokyo quaked. The dinosaurish King Zor made a bellowing sound as it rumbled around, shooting plastic balls out of its back.

In 1963 Marx introduced Big Loo, a moon robot fully a yard tall with a whole repertory of sounds and weapons. Big Loo shot both darts and water from his chest and said 10 different phrases, in addition to making bell-like, whistling, and clicking noises.

Mattel made a Lost in Space set that included a motorized Space Chariot, and Major Matt Mason, "the adventurous astronaut who lives, works and completes courageous assignments in the Mattel Space Complex!" Major Matt came with a Space Sled, a Motorized Space Crawler, a Jet Propulsion Pak, and a Cat Trac space tractor. Six inches high, Mattel's astronaut had an imposing helmet and a "flexible space suit that bends to any position."

Encouraged by the success of this entry into the space race, Mattel introduced 13-inch Captain Lazer the following year, 1968. Captain Lazer lit up like a Christmas tree: eyes, chest, even his decoder. He also made a buzzing noise.

Sears offered its own Spaceman and his best friend, Space Mutt – both wore helmets – in 1966. Then came Z-Man, a foot-long car that could be programmed to move in different directions, evade obstacles, and fire missiles, all with the help of two battery-operated motors. Amsco's entry into the mini-arms race was the Alpha-1 Ballistic Missile, which took off by water or compressed-air propulsion from a remote launching pad.

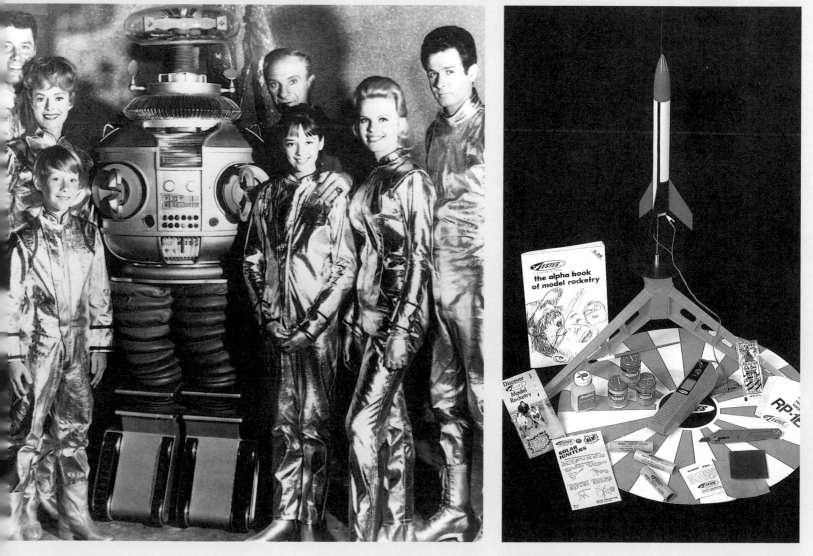

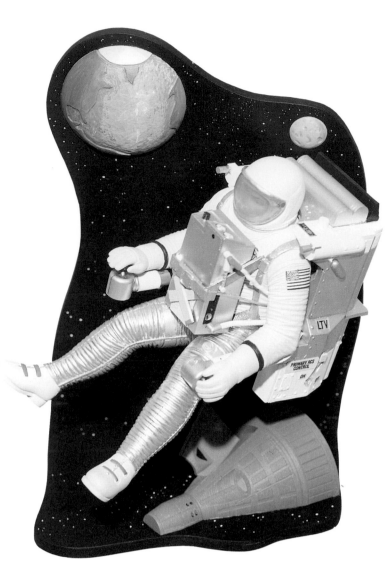

Aurora came up with the American Astronaut hobby kit ("now being launched at hobby counters everywhere"), and Transogram's Operation Orbit worked like a predecessor of the video game, with controls to land "rockets" on moving planets. In 1968 Marx brought out its Johnny Apollo Playset with "authentic astronaut equipment" including helmet, backpack, air conditioning unit, guidance gun, clipboard, cap, and tools.

Hanna-Barbera's cartoon spoof of all the space stuff – "The Jetsons" – debuted in 1962 and ran for a year, then went into syndication forever. The Jetsons had a robot maid named Rosie, who did all the household chores, and they flew around in little space cars that still managed to get into traffic jams. Knickerbocker ("Joy of a Toy") produced Rosie as a puppet, and Louis Marx made a Jetsons Turnover Tank. So durable were the original 24 animated segments that the producers finally made 41 brand-new episodes in the 1980s.

In 1977, the Hollywood blockbuster *Star Wars* reintroduced the final frontier to a new generation being raised in the video age. Between 1977 and 1984, Kenner and the other principal Star Wars toymaker, MPC, sold an unbelievable 300 million toys of every size, shape, and degree of complexity. Robots were back in business with the popularity of R2D2 and C3PO, and Hasbro's inventive Transformer toys, from 1987 on, added another dimension. These colorful, detailed robots – introduced with their own TV cartoon series – could be easily transformed into toys that had never gone out of style: cars, trucks, and planes. The wheel had come full circle.

TOP LEFT: **With Aurora's American Astronaut hobby kit, you could build and launch your own spaceman.**

RIGHT: **Ideal's Astro Rocket set.**

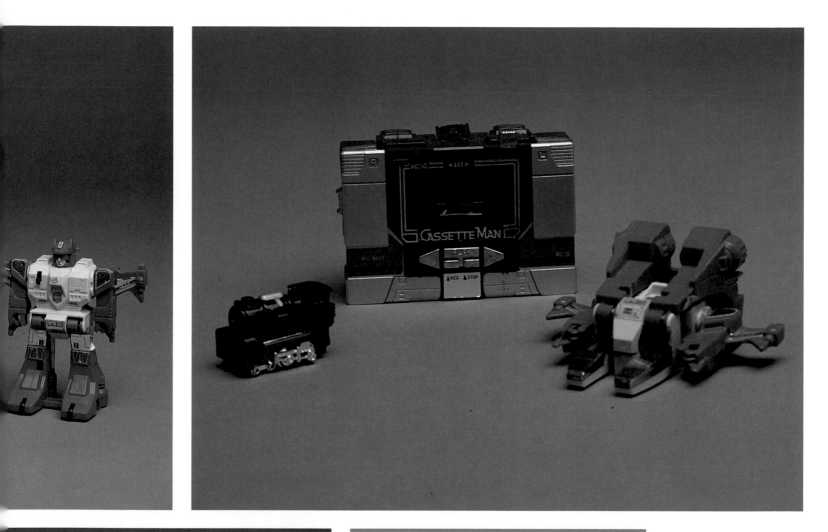

TOP CENTER AND ABOVE: **Robots still fascinate kids today, as proven by the popularity of Hasbro's innovative Transformer toys, shown "before" and "after".**

LEFT: **Space entered the video age in 1977 with George Lucas's box-office smash *Star Wars*. The film and its sequels created a toy sub-industry with more than 300 million items.**

119

Americans have always had a passion for mobility, and the transportation toys of the baby boom years seemed to encapsulate our whole history as a people on the go. From sailing ship models and covered wagons to Hot Wheels and luxury aircraft, the toymakers reflected our enduring fascination with movement.

Lionel Trains led the way into the postwar era as the world's biggest toy company. Lionel Manufacturing had been founded in 1900 by a New York inventor named Joshua Lionel Cowen, who made his first toy train to call attention to products in a toy store window. So many customers bought the "Electric Express" display piece that Cowen finally had to make a dozen more for the shopkeeper. This prototype was powered by dry-cell batteries that were wired to the track, not to the car.

Lionel's first catalog, in 1902, showed not only the Electric Express, but a two-foot-long suspension bridge, a track with a switch, a crossover track for making a figure-eight layout, and other accessories that would allow purchasers to join the ranks of the great railroad tycoons. It was the shape of things to come, not only from Lionel, but also from American Flyer, Dowst (later Tootsietoy), Ives, Marx, and others. From 1902 Lionel trains (and toy trolleys) could be operated either by batteries or by household electric current.

Before World War II, electric trains were running on three-rail systems like Lionel's. (Two rails were introduced by American Flyer after the war.) HO was the smallest of the three most common gauges of model trains, folowed by O, the mid-size gauge, and Standard (S), which was

LEFT: **American Flyers at A. C. Gilbert's New Haven, CT, factory are tested out for the 1945 holiday season.**

RIGHT: **Lionel's Pennsylvania Railroad switching engine with electrified couplers.**

BOTTOM LEFT: **Happiness is watching smoke rise from the stack of "The General," Lionel's replica of a famous wood-burning Civil War train.**

BELOW: **The ageless appeal of toy trains, as seen in a Boston department store at Christmastime in 1951.**

the largest. HO bcame increasingly popular after the war, when the new improved plastics made it possible to produce increasingly detailed sets in precise scale. Kids and dads became equally avid model railroaders.

Steam engines, diesels, work trains, passenger cars, and tenders, flashed by at bewildering speed. Cattle cars disgorged little cows, and elaborate cranes with moving parts loaded and unloaded the freight cars. Around and among the tracks sprang up entire villges, farms, and even newly developed shopping centers. Plasticville, U.S.A., from Bachman Bros. ("Makes your train set more complete") offered all of them, along with a Train Accessories Unit available for only $2.50 in 1952. According to the company's catalog, it included: "1 railroad station, 1 freight station, 2 railroad crossing gates, 4 telephone poles, 2 billboards, 2 street lamps, 1 evergreen tree and 2 benches."

American Flyer (later acquired by Lionel) offered its own Railroad Post Office to move the toy mail and an Animated Station that vibrated commuters off and onto the trains. The Talking Station called out the main stops just like a conductor would, announcing "American Flyer through train, all aboard!" Lionel introduced a micro-chip device called Rail-Sounds that incorporated the recorded sounds of real locomotives in the engine.

LIONEL

NOT JUST A TOY, A TRADITION.™

ABOVE: **A Lionel Hudson-type steam locomotive.**

SANTA FE

SANTA FE

GRANDFATHERS of America

Merry Christmas TO *Tony* FROM *Grandpop*

...selves to your mind, but somewhere a boy is dreaming of owning a ...train this Christmas. A score of other delightful gifts may present half a century, that no gift in the world so stirs his imagination as the gift of a swiftly moving LIONEL—with its realistic puffs of smoke, and its exciting whistle.

No other gift so completely carries him off into the magic-land of make-believe. It may be, too, that the boy in you will find you sprawling on the floor with him this Christmas Day—two fascinated LIONEL railroaders, both young in heart. (May we suggest that you send for the LIONEL catalog?)

Send for Color Catalog —and Book on Model R. R. Scenery Building

Catalog illustrates and describes in detail all trains and accessories.

The Lionel Corporation, Dept. D
15 East 26th Street, New York 10, N. Y.

Please send me the 1946 LIONEL full-color catalog, and book on Scenery Building. (I enclose 10c for mailing charges).

NAME _____
ADDRESS _____
_____ ZONE ____ STATE ____
(...iling.)

LIONEL TRAINS

SANTA FE

TOP LEFT: **An early color ad for Lionel trains by R. J. Tyrrell.**

TOP CENTER: **Post World War II American Flyer locomotives.**

CENTER: **American Flyer cattle car set.**

ABOVE: **A Lionel ad for the 1946 holiday season.**

LEFT: **The classic Lionel Santa Fe F3, reintroduced in 1990 with diesel sound.**

123

Toy railroads fell upon hard times during the late 1950s, when space toys and other new playthings came to the fore. Lionel tried to cope by introducing a pink-and-blue girls' set that sold – poorly – in 1957 for $37.95. Brothers, and fathers (who did most of the buying) looked askance, but by 1990 this pastel model was worth up to $1500 to collectors. Now a rejuvenated Lionel has reintroduced the ill-fated Girls' Train to its O Gauge Collector line, along with the Southern Pacific Daylight GS-2 locomotive and tender, Santa Fe F3 with aluminum cars and diesel engine, and the Pennsy S-2 Turbine – the largest locomotive ever offered by Lionel.

Louis Marx steamed through the Depression years with his popular Honeymoon Express, a colorful litho wind-up with a three-car train, station and tunnels, signaling flagman, plus farm scenes. During the 1950s, this durable toy was updated as the Mickey Mouse Express, in vibrant red, yellow, and blue, complete with a tiny airport and prop plane. Marx also produced a Union Station that whistled. His electric train sets – at budget prices, as usual – ran on three rails well into the 1950s.

In Great Britain, Wenman Bassett-Lowke, of the Northampton engineering family, introduced small-scale, prototype-modeled railway equipment after he attended the Paris Exposition of 1900 and became fascinated with the German scale-model trains from the Nuremberg firms of Bing and Märklin. Frank Hornby, the founder of Meccano Ltd., introduced the first Hornby toy train, made in Liverpool, in 1920. His colorful models were highly prized by British children, but it was not until 1938 that Hornby produced a scale-model train: the 4-6-2 *Princess Elizabeth*. After the hardships and shortages imposed by World War II, Rovex Plastics Ltd. of Richmond enjoyed immediate success with a new OO gauge train set that eventuated in the ever-expanding Tri-ang Railways line. By 1964, the Tri-ang Group had acquired the Hornby line along with Meccano Ltd. Ten years later, the renamed Hornby Railways had resumed its rightful place in British model railroading.

LEFT: **Marx's electric trains were designed for use on three-rail layouts.**

ABOVE: **The pastel Girls' Train introduced by Lionel in 1957 and reprised in the 1990 O Gauge Collectors Line.**

TOP NEAR RIGHT: **Lionel rolling stock, including passenger, freight, and tank cars.**

TOP FAR RIGHT: **Detailed Lionel accessories add depth and realism to the model railroad.**

RIGHT: **Tri-ang Railways Transcontinental Series layout, 1959.**

Cars and trucks, construction vehicles, motorcycles – and more – helped speed transportation toys into the new era. They came in metal, rubber, aluminum, plastic, tin, and composition. They represented every kind of contemporary vehicle, including some that are now just a memory. After the war, Lee Stokes Industries sold 31 different model automobiles, including DeSoto, Buick, Plymouth, Frazer, Chrysler, and Studebaker.

There were "crazy cars" like Unique's wind-up Rodeo Joe Whoopee Car and Marx's Milton Berle Car, in which the king of television comedy went round and round under the slogan "Whirl with Berle." Long before the action figure appeared, G.I. Joe and his Jouncing Jeep bounced through the postwar years "jet propelled" by a wind-up key.

Keystone made a detailed garage/service center in the late 1940s, complete with a squat gas pump of the day and "Two Keystone Automobiles with Gas Tanks That Can Be Filled." In 1954 Marx offered a Metal Service Station with accessories including grease and wash racks, cars and snap-on wheels, tool bench, bucket and sponge, air pump, grease pump – even a toilet for the restroom. Marx's familiar slogan appeared on the package: "One of the Many MARX Toys – Have You All of Them?" You were motivated to check it out at the local toy store.

Marx also offered a Pet Shop Delivery Truck with lift sides and compartments for rubber boxers, dachshunds, and cocker spaniels. His Lazy Day Farms Truck, with slatted sides, had a sign that pictured a Jersey cow with the legend "Registered Stock." The heavy-duty black plastic tires were marked "Lumar" for a realistic touch. The Marx Fire Station had two metal doors that raised and lowered; the fire truck came out when you

ABOVE: **Packaging for Doepke's streamlined miniature Jaguar.**

TOP CENTER: **Doepke's Model Toys were famous for their fidelity to their lifesize counterparts. Shown here are the Jaguar and MG.**

TOP RIGHT: **"Smitty's Toys" postwar tow truck of cast metal and aluminum.**

RIGHT: **Rugged Buddy L and Tonka steel fire trucks in true fire-engine red.**

126

turned a crank on the side. Accessories included everything but a Dalmatian – perhaps overlooked by the Marx engineering department at the design stage.

Structo had been making pressed-steel vehicles since the twenties, and they were still well represented in the mid-1950s toy catalogs. The company made realistic-looking cars, trucks, farm, and construction toys that were designed and painted to last. Dent had made cast-iron toys before they became uneconomical, and the company's reputation for quality was high. It was among the first to produce toy planes like the 1932 Air Express in olive, silver, red, and gold. Dent also made cars, cabs, fire engines – even zeppelins. Later they shifted to aluminum toys, but these were not as well received by kids who were used to hefting the heavier metal vehicles. Aluminum didn't seem as substantial.

Buddy L pressed-steel toys were known for their accuracy, size, and durability. And no wonder. They were designed by Fred Lundhal, owner of the Moline (Illinois) Pressed Steel Company, for his son Buddy, who was going through a lot of flimsier toys that kept on breaking. The first all-steel Buddy L truck was two feet long. You could jump up and down on it without the least effect. This tradition has continued into the present, through a long line of Buddy L nearly indestructible cars, trucks, and construction equipment.

Doepke's Model Toys (primarily steel reproductions of heavy construction equipment) have been called "the finest line of toys of the post-war era." Each toy was authorized by the "lifesize" manufacturer and conformed perfectly to its equipment. There was a working Barber-Greene high-capacity bucket loader, Adams diesel road graders with adjustable blades, and Heiliner earth scrapers correct to the last detail of color, tread, and tire size. Expensive as they were compared to other toys of the kind, Doepke's were steady sellers. They came with everything but hard hats and construction permits.

Smith-Miller was another postwar toymaker dedicated to crafting perfect duplicates. Their trucks and tractors, made of cast metal and aluminum, were advertised with the slogan "Cost More Because They Give More." Smitty's Toys, as they were affectionately called, did offer value for money – right up to the aerial ladder truck at a then-astronomical $27.85.

Tru-Miniatures lived up to its name with a steady flow of toy cars and trucks designed to look like the real thing, and Hubley maintained its long-time reputation despite the metal shortages reimposed by the Korean War of the early 1950s. At that time, Hubley admitted that it was exploring the field of plastic toys, but by 1955 it was happily concentrating again on the well-made metal models that had made the company famous. These included taxis and warplanes – folding-wing prop planes and a Folding Wing Jet with retractable landing gear, brilliantly painted in red and gold.

Some of the higher-priced metal trucks and cars were affected by the success of less detailed – and less expensive – products from emerging companies like Tonka

TOP LEFT: **Tonka's steel mini dump truck offered competition to other miniature toy vehicles such as Matchbox.**

MIDDLE LEFT: **Volkswagen Beetle models from various manufacturers, 1950s-early 1970s.**

TOP: **Tonka's indestructible steel trucks were especially entertaining in a sandbox.**

ABOVE: **The hydraulic dump truck offered by Tonka in the 1960s.**

LEFT: **A kid-sized 1956 Pontiac convertible.**

and Nylint. Their steel models were both tough and good-looking, and they won a big following during the 1950s. Tonka Toys' Mighty Dump and Volkswagen Beetle models were especially popular. Ertl, too, had found a secure niche for its steel products, especially farm vehicles, by the late 1950s. Founder Fred Ertl, Sr., of Dubuque, Iowa, contracted with manufacturers like John Deere and International Harvester (whose blueprints he used for copies) to unveil his models at the same time they showed their new lines to the farm trade. Now Ertl is the world's biggest manufacturer of toy farm equipment, along with other vehicles including cars, trucks, and planes.

Topper rumbled onto the truck scene with its Johnny Express Tractor Trailer – a huge toy operated by remote-control levers. During the late 1960s, Topper would challenge Mattel's pre-eminent Hot Wheels cars and tracks, billed as "The Fastest Cars in the World!" These HO-scaled racing cars were gravity powered and came with a plastic track that could be bent or looped without throwing off the cars, which traveled upside-down and sideways too. From the first-edition "California Custom Styling" models with their "dazzling Spectraflame paint jobs," to custom Cougars, T-Birds, and El Dorados, Mattel had the inside track on miniature metal racers from 1968 on. Topper's Johnny Lightning Jet-power Cars never did catch up with Mattel, despite such hot models as the Fabulous Fin, Flying Needle, Screamer, and Manta Ray.

TOP LEFT: **Lesney's brilliant line of 1:75-scale Matchbox miniature vehicles zoomed into the U.S. in the 1950s to instant acclaim.**

BOTTOM LEFT: **This Matchbox Series Gift Set included a nifty car transporter and a boat with trailer.**

LEFT: **Lesney's packaging has always been as meticulous as its products.**

TOP CENTER: **More Matchbox cars, trucks, vans, and sedans to gladden a collector's heart.**

ABOVE: **Classic cars of yesteryear are integral to the Matchbox line.**

The British were coming throughout the 1950s and 1960s, with such quality entries as Lesney's famous Matchbox line of 1:75-scale miniature cars. Packaged in the readily identified little cardboard boxes that gave the toy its name, the tiny autos, trucks, tractors, emergency vehicles, and buses were an immediate – and enduring – success. Soon there were blue carrying cases for kid collectors who had scooped up dozens of Matchbox vehicles. Then Welsh manufacturer Mettoy went smaller with its popular Corgi cars and introduced them as the Husky line, later re-named Corgi Junior.

Corgi, in turn, had started out as Mettoy's answer to Dinky Toys, then England's best-selling line of toy cars. Dinky also made planes, boats, and other vehicles that have become collectors' items since it went out of business.

LEFT: **Mettoy, of Wales, makes the popular Corgi line of miniature vehicles.**

ABOVE: **A selection of Dinky Toys of the 1950s and 1960s.**

LEFT: **Dinky Toys were once the best-selling toy vehicles in the U.K.**

RIGHT: **Now collectors' items, Dinky Toys are auctioned at Christie's.**

Both domestic and imported wheels had to contend with the slot-car racing craze that began in 1962 and peaked in the early 1970s. Like model trains, slot cars were powered by electric transformers that sent current to the slots inset into the "racetrack." Speed was controlled by separate hand controls for each "driver," which grew more sophisticated with time. By the mid-1960s, when Cox introduced slot cars to its line, the country had gone slot-car crazy, not only with home sets, but on storefront tracks where drivers challenged each other on multilane courses.

Aurora Plastics was instrumental in starting the trend with its high-powered Ford Grand National Model Motoring Competition in 1962. More than a million contestants signed up, and public interest was fanned by a story in *Look* magazine. Other enterprising toymakers soon started their engines.

Ideal offered a Torture Track for its Motorific cars, and Revell had slot-car layouts like Enduro, Gran Turismo, Europa, and Americana. Mattel's Switch 'n' Go cars, Tyco's HO-scale TycoPro line, Strombecker's reasonably priced road racers – all had their day in the sun.

The late 1960s and early 1970s brought Kenner's Super Sonic Power (SSP) cars. Unlike the slot-cars, they operated on a simple gyro-wheel principle that was activated by a ratcheted T-Handle Power Stick. You inserted the stick into the flywheel in the car's base and yanked it out. Made of plastic, the sturdy cars came in a range of designs, from realistic to fantastic.

Kenner got fancy with the Drag Race Set Unlimited, whose finish-line wire triggered off a parachute that ballooned out behind the triumphant dragster. For its popular SSP Smash-Up Derby set, the cars were designed to fly to pieces on impact, as in a real demolition derby. The SSP line became the best-selling boys' toy of the early 1970s.

Another fad of the era combined the fascination of "funny cars" and monsters beginning in 1963. Model-maker Revell got together with cartoonist Ed Roth and the result was a line of offbeat dragsters and hot rods driven by monsters with names like Ratfink. The idea caught on, and the Hawk Model Company came out with its Weird-Oh line, including Davey the Psycho Cyclist. In the late 1960s, Revell went to fantasy-car illustrator Dave Deal for a new line, called Deal's Wheels, that put more emphasis on the cars themselves. Two of Deal's most popular designs were wacked-out Volkswagens: The Bug Bomb and the Glitter Bug. When the furor died down, Revell went back to making the accurate scale-models of popular and classic cars that had been its mainstay since 1950.

Meanwhile, other nonexotic cars, trucks, and accessories had never gone out of style. Would-be mechanics were delighted with Ideal's red-and-blue plastic Fix-It Truck with removable wheels and spare tire. It came with a tool box complete with lift-jack, screwdriver, wrench, and hammer. Nosco Plastics produced a popular friction-motor Cop-Cycle with sidecar. Amsco came up with the Magic Gas Pump, which appeared to pour and measure gasoline and then refill itself. And the Tootsietoy Super Service Station of the 1960s was complete to the last detail – and portable as well.

136

LEFT: **Everyone got into the groove with slot-car racing, seen here on a 1966 Lionel layout.**

ABOVE: **Kenner Products' fly-apart/put-together Smash-up Derby Set.**

LEFT: **Mattel's gravity-powered Hot Wheels racers took on all comers as "the fastest cars in the world!"**

BELOW: **An A. C. Gilbert entry in the slot-car racing field.**

ABOVE: **Roller skating was all the rage in the 1950s.**

TOP RIGHT: **British ride-size toys included this elegant Austin in robin's-egg blue.**

RIGHT: **Winter wouldn't have been the same without a Flexible Flyer sled.**

FAR RIGHT: **The classic little red wagon, by Radio Flyer, was the perfect vehicle for a Sunday drive – if you could get your little brother to push.**

THE BLUE ANGELS

U.S. NAVY

Blue Angels

Latest in the series of outstanding planes flown by the world famous U.S. Navy Blue Angels flight team is the blazing McDonnell Douglas Phantom II. Aurora's 1/48 scale kit version includes detailed landing gear and cockpit, sidewinder missiles, display stand, and special full color decals to enable the model builder to construct any Phantom II in the Blue Angel team. $2.50 Retail

No. 367 THE BLUE ANGELS PHANTOM II
Carton Pack: 1 dozen Carton Weight: 12 lbs.

AURORA made the going great with its PAN-AM 747...
Then we flew the friendly skies with our United 747...

NEW

NOW, "Delta is ready when you are" with AURORA'S NEW DELTA 747...

NEW

AND, "It's up, up, and away" with AURORA'S NEW TWA 747

More advertising has been focused on the 747 than any product in history. Take full advantage with Aurora's giant 15″ wingspan kits, now from four airlines.

KIT NO.	KIT NAME	CARTON PACK	CARTON WT.	RETAIL
360	DELTA 747	12	12 lbs.	$2.50
361	PAN AM 747	12	12 lbs.	2.50
362	UNITED 747	12	12 lbs.	2.50
363	TWA 747	12	12 lbs.	2.50

NEW (360)
NEW (363)

AURORA

AURORA PRODUCTS CORP., 44 CHERRY VALLEY ROAD, WEST HEMPSTEAD, N.Y. 11552
PRINTED IN U.S.A.

ABOVE: **Aurora's 1:48-scale model McDonnell Douglas Phantom II, flown by the U.S. Navy Blue Angels flight team.**

RIGHT: **Kusan Toys' Ride 'Em Jet, 1971.**

ABOVE RIGHT: **Trade ad for Aurora's Delta and TWA 747 model airplane kits.**

American

CLEVELAND

BIG TICKET kits timed right for Xmas.

This sleek single-seater had just what the big Air Force ordered—speed, maneuverability, and especially easy assembly. With big easy-to-handle parts for simple no-nonsense assembly.

No. 377 P-51 MUSTANG
Wingspan 16"
$3.50 retail
Carton Pack: 1 Dozen   Carton Weight: 14 Lbs.

TWO MORE WINNERS IN AURORA'S SCREWDRIVER SERIES

deserved the adjective "legendary." It's the P-40 of Road and made possible the airlifting of supplies to ries. Another easy-to-assemble model in Aurora's best-

No. 378 CURTIS P-40
Wingspan 16"
$3.50 retail
Carton Pack: 1 Dozen   Carton Weight: 14 Lbs.

© Aurora Plastics Corp., West Hempstead, N.Y. 11552

ABOVE: **Holiday trade ad for Aurora's P-51 Mustang and Curtis P-40 kits.**

TOP RIGHT: **P-38 and B-25 plastic bombers from Renwal.**

LEFT: **No thrill like test-piloting your own remote-control helicopter with Marilyn Products' pylon and airport – 1955.**

Tootsietoy had been important in toy planes, as well as cars, for generations. The company's excellent designs and packaging, combined with low prices, made them favorites with kids who eagerly collected the Ford Trimotor Airport and the six-piece "Aeroplane" set of the early 1940s. Strombecker's precut wooden models, like the Boeing B-29 Superfortress, were especially popular during World War II. The company thrived through the metal-shortage years and won fans among boys who had been confirmed Hubley buyers.

Guillow's soared high on the wings of its popular balsa wood gliders, including the early 1950s USAF Starfire and SkyStreak models that have remained unchanged to this day. The company has added some space shuttles and the like as a concession to the space age, but its most durable models look just like the ones we flew.

The 1950s were boom years for build-it-yourself plastic models, thanks in part to improved plastic cements. Monogram, Aurora, and Pyro were big names, and Revell was the biggest of all. By the mid-1950s, Revell was producing more planes than the entire air industry.

Cox offered an exciting assortment of gas-powered planes for older kids, some of them based on fighter planes from World War II, like the Stuka Dive Bomber and the P-40 Flying Tiger. In the late 1960s, the company introduced motorized model rockets and rocketry kits. Cox reminded hobbyists in its advertising that "You can't get this kind of go with power cells or batteries. You need the real thing: a gas engine." By this time (1971), a lot of baby boomers were even more interested in the gas engine that ran the family car, since they were old enough to drive. Some were even old enough to fly.

Even little kids showed an interest in aerodynamics. Fisher-Price made a fleet of study airliners, from the Play Family Fun Jet to the Woodsey's Airport Set, with its foam-rubber plane and finger-pupper pilot, Uncle Filbert (a squirrel). Older air aces went for the Hubley die-cast P-38s with folding landing gear, which were sold from the 1940s into the 1970s. The ever-increasing popularity of air travel resulted in luxury models like Schuco's Lufthansa Airliner. By the mid-1970s, American mobility could be measured at the speed of sound, and a whole generation was ready for take-off.

By the early 1950s, toys based on popular characters were booming, thanks to the combined forces of radio, comic-strips, comic-books, movies, children's magazines and pulp novels, and especially, television. Many a character who had started out in the 1920s and 1930s as a comic-strip cartoon found himself singing, dancing, and telling stories to an audience of millions, as television antennas sprang up across the land. Toymakers were among the chief beneficiaries.

Disney toys had been coming on line since the advent of Mickey Mouse in *Steamboat Willie*, the sound short released by the Disney Studios in November 1928. Mickey was an immediate hit, and the first doll in his image appeared in 1930. Despite the Depression, 15 other Mickey Mouse toys came out the following year, and after that they just kept on coming. There was a Wood Dancer on strings, a metal drum, a sparkler, a wooden squeak toy, a Tumbling Circus Toy, and several games. A year later, toy distributor George Borgfeldt advertised Mickey Mouse playthings as the "Toy and Specialty items that have become the favorites of millions – adults and children." That pretty much covered it.

Minnie Mouse, who had also debuted in *Steamboat Willie*, first appeared as a doll in 1931, soon followed by Donald Duck, Pluto and Goofy, the Three Little Pigs, and the Big Bad Wolf. Many toymakers survived the Depression only with the help of Mickey Mouse and his friends. Lionel Trains credits Mickey with keeping it on the rails with the famous Mickey Mouse Handcar, which came out in 1935. Other manufacturers had cause to bless the name of Walt Disney too.

As Disney animated classics like *Snow White and the Seven Dwarfs* continued to emerge from the studio, Disney toys increased and multiplied. Some manufacturers made nothing but Disney-license playthings. Fun-E-Flex's whole line consisted of two items: jointed wooden Mickeys and Minnies, four inches high, with leather ears, arms, legs, and tails.

Fisher-Price wheeled out an endless line of engaging Disney pull toys for tots who could say "Mickey" almost as soon as "Mommy." There was a Donald Duck Choo-Choo; a Mickey Mouse drummer; a Donald Duck Xylophone, with seven keys energetically played by the irascible duck himself; a Mickey Mouse Choo-Choo with a bell on top (not just window dressing – it really made noise, like most Fisher-Price items); a Mickey Mouse Puddle Jumper (with clacker), and more.

When *Pinocchio* was released by Disney in 1940, there was a run on Jiminy Crickets, Monstro the Whales, Gepettos like Pinocchio's "father," the puppetmaker, and the long-nosed puppet himself. Ideal offered a jointed Pinocchio of painted wood, and Louis Marx, inevitably, created a wind-up toy. Of course, classic characters got a new lease on life as toys when they starred in Disney movies like *Alice in Wonderland, Bambi, Peter Pan, Winnie the Pooh, The Jungle Book, Cinderella*, and, more recently, *The Little Mermaid* and *Beauty and the Beast*.

The 1950s "Disneyland" TV show, and the Disney theme parks, Disneyland and Walt Disney World, have only increased the demand for the ever-growing list of toys kids can't live without. It seems appropriate

BELOW: **The mouse who started it all: Walt Disney's Mickey in** *Steamboat Willie* **(1928). His trademark white gloves were added later.**

RIGHT: **Packaging for Parker Brothers' Disney-licensed Mickey Mouse Comic Picture puzzle.**

BOTTOM RIGHT: **The 12-panel Mickey Mouse Comic Picture Puzzle from Parker Brothers.**

ABOVE: **Walt Disney Mickey Mouse Band pull toy, with cymbal on Pluto's tail.**

ABOVE RIGHT: **Early Disney character dolls – Goofy, Pinocchio, Donald, and Minnie.**

RIGHT: **The unforgettable Mouseketeers, on the long-running "Mickey Mouse Club" TV series.**

LEFT: **Vintage cartoon character dolls, including Mickey, Minnie, Pinocchio, and the Big Bad Wolf; Little Lulu; and Tom and Jerry.**

that Lionel celebrated the 1990 anniversary of Walt Disney World with a special 20th Anniversary Train Set – and a Mickey Mouse & Donald Duck Handcar.

That pipe-clenching old salt Popeye first appeared in 1929, in E.C. Segar's "Thimble Theatre" comic-strip. At first, he was a minor character, but public demand soon put him in the spotlight – along with Wimpy, Olive Oyl, and baby Sweet Pea. During the 1930s, Hubley produced a cast-iron Popeye Patrol motorcycle, and the famous biceps were displayed to good advantage in Marx's Popeye the Champ wind-up – a boxing ring set-up not dissimilar to the later Rock 'Em Sock 'Em Robot set. Chein made several wind-up Popeye Punchers, with a punching bag suspended in front of the tattooed sailor man. There was a Thimble Theatre Mystery Playhouse from Harding Products and two Popeye Express sets from Marx. Metal Masters created a Popeye and Sweet Pea Xylophone, Linemar launched Popeye on Roller Skates, and Hasbro even made a Popeye Gumball Machine.

The King Features TV series kept Popeye in the public eye right through the 1960s. Mattel made a Popeye "Getar" Ukulele – strummable or crankable – that played (good guess) "Popeye the Sailor Man," and Elm Toys put Popeye, Wimpy, Olive, and Bluto into sportscars. Although his popularity has waned since then, Popeye is still one of the best-recognized cartoon characters of all time.

FAR LEFT: **The delightful Mickey Mouse Club stuffed car with Pluto klaxon.**

ABOVE: **Colorforms' Mickey Mouse Pop-up Playset.**

LEFT: **Goofy dispenser for Pez candies. Pez dispensers were, and still are, highly collectable.**

RIGHT: **The Mickey Mouse Club TV Playhouse.**

The 1950s were the heyday of the "Howdy Doody Show" and all its offspring. From 1947 to 1960, you could visit Doodyville every week on NBC-TV to watch "Buffalo Bob" Smith orchestrate his cast of marionettes. With him were Don Knotts, who played both Tim Tremble and Chief Thunderthud, and Bob Keeshan, who played Clara Hornblow, the cow with the seltzer squirter, before going on to fame and fortune as Captain Kangaroo.

Howdy himself was a jug-eared, freckly marionette who would be immortalized by the Kagren Company, which produced seven of the show's characters, strings and all, so that kids could put on their own shows. In addition to the Kagren marionettes – including Phineas T. Bluster, Dilly Dally, Flub-a-dub, Princess Summer-Fall-Winter-Spring, and Heidi Doody – you could get Unique Art's Howdy Doody Band. There were also the wood-and-plastic animated toys, including the Howdy Phone-a-Doodle and the memorable Clock-a-Doodle, in which Howdy swung from the pendulum and the disheveled Flub-a-dub popped out on the hour, like a cuckoo. It was fun.

From 1948 to the late 1950s, the popular "Kukla, Fran & Ollie" series transported kids to a delightful realm populated by the Kuklapolitan puppet company. Puppeteer Burr Tillstrom and the engaging Fran Allison – only two humans appeared – brought out the best in their cast. Kukla (from the Russian diminutive for "doll") had a clown nose and a running repartee with Ollie, a velvet dragon with a single pointed tooth, who sometimes got out of hand. Other characters who came to life again as plush dolls and hand puppets you could take home included Madame Ophelia Oglepuss, Beulah Witch, and Fletcher Rabbit.

ABOVE: **The delightful Kukla and Ollie the Dragon puppets, of the popular "Kukla, Fran and Ollie" children's TV show.**

TOP RIGHT: **Howdy Doody enlisted in the cause of literacy on the memorable "Howdy Doody Show."**

RIGHT: **After a while, Buffalo Bob started looking a lot like Howdy and Heidi.**

FAR RIGHT: **"Buffalo Bob" Smith, Howdy, and Clarabell the Clown celebrate 10 years on television in 1957.**

ABOVE: **A comic Popeye puzzle with Olive Oyl, baby Wimpy, and rival Bluto.**

NEAR RIGHT: **Castle Films' production of** *Howdy Doody's Christmas,* **for home viewing.**

TOP RIGHT: **With your own Howdy Doody puppets, you could put on your own Howdy Doody show.**

FAR RIGHT: **The pugnacious Popeye starred in Louis Marx's Popeye the Champ wind-up toy.**

LEFT: **A Bert puppet of "Sesame Street" fame gets his nose tweaked by an enthusiastic fan.**

ABOVE: **Count von Count made learning numbers child's play on "Sesame Street."**

BELOW: **The original cast of "Sesame Street."**

"Sesame Street" started its long run on PBS in 1969 with a lively mix of puppets and people, directed to preschool-age children. This groundbreaking show used the techniques and pacing of commercial television to teach numbers, letters, and values not only painlessly, but entertainingly. Jim Henson's Muppets captivated both kids and parents with their true-to-life activities, problems, and delights. Bert and Ernie, Big Bird, the Cookie Monster, and Oscar the Grouch, who lived in a garbage can, inspired a host of popular toys.

Topper's Big Bird, unmistakably yellow, had plastic eyes and feet, a flexible vinyl beak, and felt "hands." You could pose him in various ways, and there was a hole in the back of his head so that you could make his beak move. Fisher-Price made an Oscar the Grouch that popped out of his garbage can when you squeezed a bulb. Also from Fisher-Price were the Sesame Street Clubhouse and the Play Family Sesame Street – a miniature block party complete with "brownstone" facades, furniture, Big Bird's nest, a sanitation truck, a lightpole with street sign, and more. The set came with eight figures, and you could get others separately, including Mr. Snuffleupagus, the elephant; scowling Herry Monster; Sherlock Hemlock; and Count von Count, an unscary vampire who helped teach numbers.

Besides Big Bird, Topper offered other puppets, the Spell-A-Phone, Walking Letters, and Sherlock Hemlock Magic Puzzles. When Jim Henson launched his own show, "The Muppets," in 1976, he introduced the immortal Miss Piggy, in perpetual pursuit of a reluctant Kermit the Frog.

Beginning in 1969, Fred Rogers wrote, produced, and performed in "Mr. Rogers' Neighborhood," a low-key, reassuring, and fun TV program for young children. The show, which emphasized values and resolving problems amicably, had its own puppet stars, including King Friday, Lady Elaine, and Owl, who were reprised by Ideal in the 1970s.

The larger-than-life Jackie Gleason, who started out as a stand-up comic in New Jersey nightclubs, began his long-running TV career as "The Great One" during the 1950s. Gleason appeared in innumerable shows, including hs own variety series in the 1960s, but he is best remembered for "The Honeymooners," aired during the 1955-56 season. This classic comedy series starred Gleason as the overbearing but irresistible Ralph Kramden, the harried Brooklyn bus driver who dreamed big dreams in the sparsely furnished kitchen that was the show's only set. Gleason was brilliantly supported by Audrey Meadows as his long-suffering wife, Alice, and Art Carney as Ed Norton, his best friend and upstairs neighbor, whom Gleason alternately abused and inspired. One of Gleason's trademark expressions – "And away-y-y we go!" – was emblazoned on Wolverine's Honeymooners Bus, which wound up and took off with Ralph at the wheel and the rest of the cast as passengers.

"The Honeymooners" was so popular that Hanna-Barbera Productions created a cartoon takeoff set in the Stone Age: "The Flintstones." Fred Flintstone and his wife, Wilma, lived in a cavelike suburban house in Bedrock near friends Barney and Betty Rubble. Their baby son Bam-Bam was a favorite with little Pebbles Flintstone. Dino, the pet dinosaur, completed the cast. "The Flintstones" aired for six years – the longest run for a prime-time animated series in TV history – and resulted in some memorable comic toys and other merchandising tie-ins, some of which are still with us.

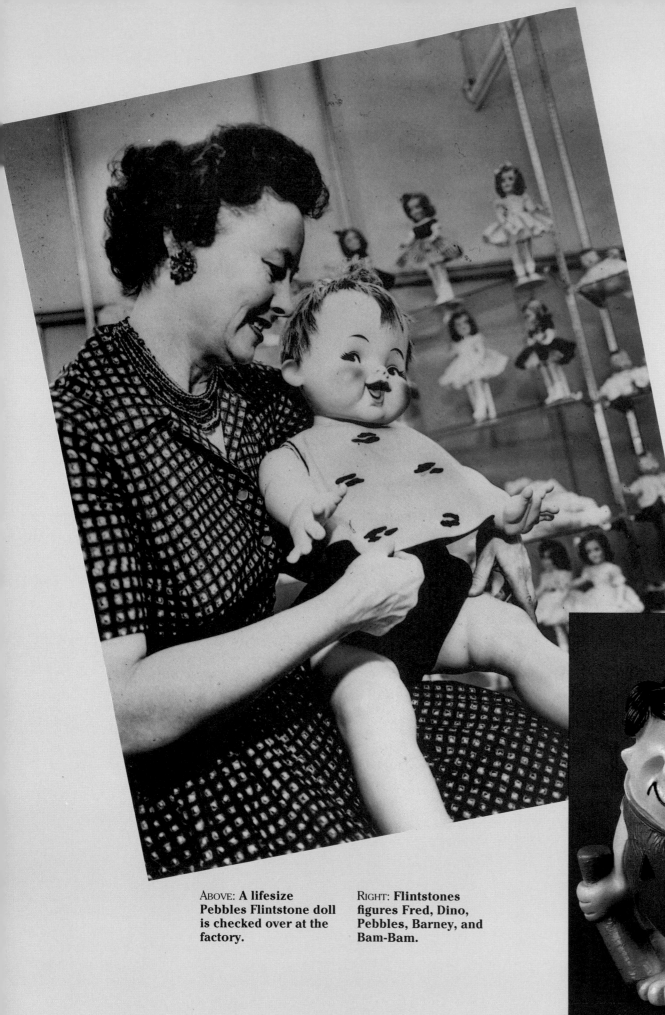

ABOVE: **A lifesize Pebbles Flintstone doll is checked over at the factory.**

RIGHT: **Flintstones figures Fred, Dino, Pebbles, Barney, and Bam-Bam.**

Linemar produced the plush-and-plastic Dino the Dinosaur and Fred Flintstone, with eight actions. Pink-and-blue Dino was ridden by Fred in something that looked like a prehistoric elephant howdah, and batteries bumped the two along. Playskool made a plastic pull toy with gigantic "stone wheels," with Fred and Barney on one side. When you flipped it over, Pebbles and Bam-Bam were in the driver's seat. There were also Flintstone trains, vinyl dolls, a shooting gallery, and a Turnover Tank that Louis Marx later recycled for "The Jetsons."

Warner Bros.' Bugs Bunny, who has been around almost as long as Mickey Mouse, never lost his popularity with kids who saw him in the classic Looney Tunes cartoons. Bugs and his friends Daffy Duck and Elmer Fudd have inspired many a toy, including Mattel's Bugs Bunny Talking Hand Puppet (with pull-string "talker" to activate the inimitable Bugs voice) and Bugs-Bunny-in-the-Music-Box.

Mattel's popular music-box line also features Charles Schulz's Snoopy, the best-selling beagle of all time, to the tune of "Where, Oh, Where Has My Little Dog Gone?" The perennial "Peanuts" strip has been around since 1950, and there's no end in sight to the toys it has created. That lovable loser Charlie Brown; Schroeder, the musical prodigy who dotes on Beethoven; Lucy, the mean big sister; Linus-and-his-blanket; that little mess, Pigpen; Woodstock, the bird, and the rest are here to stay. Snoopy leads the toy parade, in his Flying Ace Biplane from Aviva, the Snoopy Copter pull toy (with Woodstock) from Hasbro, and others too numerous to list. Other characters appear in playsets such as Questor's Camp Kamp, with cabin and bunk beds, picnic table, and canoe.

SNOOPY Copter

Pull Toy

ROMPER ROOM

17

RIGHT: Romper Room catalog page of Snoopy toys.

TOP CENTER: Gumby's pal Pokey the Pony as a hand puppet from Lakeside.

FAR RIGHT: The indestructible Gumby himself as a hand puppet. The familiar Gumby dolls came later.

822 SNOOPY Copter   Ages: 1 to 4

A unique sound and action pull toy features SNOOPY and his pal WOODSTOCK

- SNOOPY's soft ears spin round 'n round like a helicopter.
- Funny boing – boing sound.

6¼ x 5¼ x 7¾"
WT.: 14 lbs.
PACK: 12 pcs.
CU.FT.: 1.8

PEANUTS Characters ⁻1958, 1955, 1966, 1972 United Feature Syndicate, Inc.

SNOOPY Jack-in-the-Box

820 SNOOPY Jack-in-the-Box   Ages: 2 to 6

The **only** jack-in-the-box with **Double Popping** action! SNO
means double th

- Turn the cra
  Beagle."
- SURPRISE! W
  his nest.
- SURPRISE! SN
  front door.

7 x 6 x 5¼"
WT.: 12 lbs.

PEANUTS Characters: ⁻19

LEFT: What would a Linus doll be without a blanket?

RIGHT: The gang's all here in this Snoopy and His Friends playset, 1958.

156

Another durable animated figure is Gumby, "the world's favorite Clay-boy," created by Art Clokey almost 30 years ago. "The Adventures of Gumby" and his claymate Pokey, the red horse, based on Clokey's stop-motion technique for making gradual changes in clay figures, now number 130, some of them available on video. The first time I saw Gumby, I thought he was an eraser. But shows like "The Fantastic Farmer" showed me what he was really all about: he may get flattened, but he always comes back. Kids – and grown-ups – can appreciate that, which is one reason Gumby and the toys he's inspired are still with us.

As the baby-boom years ended, toys based on cartoon figures represented a huge segment of the business – a third of all the toys produced. Fad games and gimmicks had come and gone; some had come and stayed. Video games were just a blip on the horizon. Toy manufacturers had emerged, folded, hung in there, retired, or quintupled their business, depending upon how well they met the needs of changing times.

And what about us? All those kids who used to be?

We're everywhere.

You can tell by the way our eyes light up when we say, "I had one of those!"

Index

Acknowledgments

The author and publisher would like to thank Barbara Guyette, the Longabucco family, Tim Oei, Harry L. Rinker, Herb Rolfes, the Schneider family, Donald Sheldon, Gary Ulery, Mike Vargas, and Andrew Yanchus for the generous use of their collections, as well as numerous toy manufacturers for a wealth of information and photographic material.

Thanks also go to the editor, Jean Martin; the picture researcher, Sara Dunphy; the designer, Adrian Hodgkins; and the indexer, Elizabeth A. McCarthy.

Picture Credits

Binney and Smith, Easton, PA: pages 11 (top right, bottom right), 50 (bottom right).
Brompton Photo Library: pages 142-143 (bottom center), 145 (bottom).
Cadaco Games, Chicago, IL: pages 31 (bottom left), 33 (top left).
Chester Toy Museum: pages 2-3 (bottom center), 22 (top left), 98 (bottom), 130-131, 135 (both).
The Children's Museum of Indianapolis/ Photography by Charlene Faris: pages 37 (top left), 49 (top right, center left), 50 (top right), 59 (top left), 62 (top left), 66-67 (top center), 70 (bottom right), 72 (bottom right), 81 (top), 87 (bottom), 95 (bottom right), 118-119 (bottom center), 124 (both), 127 (bottom), 128 (center right).
Courtesy Christie's, South Kensington: pages 102-103 (top center), 114 (left), 133 (both), 134.
Courtesy Classic Toy Train Magazine: pages 122-123 (bottom center, top center, center, left center).
Daisy Air Rifles: page 91.
Estes Industries Hi-Flier Manufacturing Co.: page 117 (bottom right).
Collection of Richard Friz: pages 40 (bottom right), 59 (bottom), 61, 73, 89 (bottom left), 94 (bottom), 104 (top left, bottom), 105 (right), 114 (center right), 139 (top), 144 (bottom), 149 (top right), 151 (top right, bottom right).
Collection of Barbara Guyette: pages 3 (bottom right), 55 (bottom left), 67 (bottom left, right), 68 (bottom), 69 (bottom left, right), 70 (left, top right), 72 (left), 77 (top right, center right), 78 (both), 81 (bottom left), 82-83, 110 (bottom right), 155 (top left), 156 (bottom left), 157 (bottom left).
Hasbro, Inc.: pages 100 (top right), 156 (top).
Hornby Hobbies, Ltd.: page 125 (bottom).
Courtesy Mrs. Betty James, James Industries, Hollidaysburg, PA: pages 10-11 (top center, bottom center), page 11 (bottom left).
Courtesy Jefferson Guitar Co.: page 58.
Jesco Doll Co.: page 71 (top).
Joy Luke Fine Arts Broker and Auctioneer, Bloomington, IL: page 144 (top).
Collection of Jeff Judson, Flemington, NJ: page 151 (top).
Kenner Products, Cincinnati, OH: pages 49 (top left), 54 (center left), 137 (top left).
Lego Systems, Inc.: pages 42, 43 (top).
Lionel Trains, Inc.: pages 122 (top left), 123 (top right).
Courtesy London Bridge Collectors Toys/ Photography by Harry L. Rinker, Jr.: pages 98 (top), 99 (top, bottom left).
Courtesy the Longabucco Family/ Photography by Roman Woloszyn: pages 21 (bottom), 24 (bottom), 34 (top right), 36 (bottom), 100-101 (bottom center, top), 118 (top right), 119 (top right), 146, 147 (top, bottom right).
Coco McCoy, Rainbow: pages 2 (center left), 48, 129 (top), 145 (top left), 153 (top left).

Courtesy Jean Martin/Photography by Roman Woloszyn: pages 52 (top right), 147 (bottom left).
Mattel Toys: pages 74-75, 76, 77 (bottom), 79, 84 (top, bottom left), 115 (right), 137 (center).
Milton Bradley Co.: pages 25 (bottom right), 26 (top left).
Courtesy Elizabeth Montgomery/ Photography by Roman Woloszyn: page 128 (top right).
Collection of Tim Oei: pages 99 (bottom right), 106 (top left), 125 (top left, right), 126 (top left), 127 (top left, right), 132 (center left, bottom left).
Ohio Art: pages 52 (top left), 64, 65 (center left).
Courtesy Parker Bros.: pages 19 (both), 27 (top).
Radio Flyer, Inc.: page 139 (bottom right).
Collection of Harry L. Rinker, Sr./ Photography by Harry L. Rinker, Jr.: pages 2 (top left), 17 (both), 21 (top right), 24 (top), 25 (top left, bottom left), 27 (center), 28 (both), 29 (both), 30 (bottom right), 32 (both), 33 (bottom left), 34 (bottom), 37 (top right), 49 (bottom), 51 (top left, right), 53 (bottom left), 54-55 (top center), 57 (bottom), 59 (top right), 68 (top), 80, 84-85 (bottom center), 88, 89 (top left), 90 (both), 94-95 (top center, bottom center), 96-97 (top center), 109 (top right), 110 (top left), 111, 119 (bottom right), 131 (bottom left), 141 (top right), 143 (top, bottom right), 150 (both), 151 (top), 155 (top right), 157 (top left, top right).
Collection of Herb Rolfes/Photography by Harry L. Rinker, Jr.: pages 38-39, 62 (bottom), 65 (bottom right), 154-155 (bottom center).
Courtesy the Schneider Family/Photography by Roman Woloszyn: pages 22 (bottom), 23 (top right), 27 (bottom), 29 (bottom), 30 (top), 31 (top left), 35 (top right), 51 (bottom left), 52 (bottom right), 53 (top), 63 (both).
Sears, Roebuck & Co.: pages 100 (left), 116 (left).
Collection of Donald Sheldon/Photography by Harry L. Rinker, Jr.: pages 108, 109 (bottom left).
Collection of Gary Ulery/Photography by Harry L. Rinker, Jr.: page 33 (bottom left).
UPI/Bettmann Newsphotos: pages 1, 4-5, 6-7, 8, 12 (top right, bottom), 13, 14, 15, 16, 18 (top left), 20 (top left), 26 (bottom left), 35 (top left, bottom), 36 (top left), 40 (top right), 41 (top right), 43 (bottom left), 44-45, 54 (bottom left, bottom right), 56-57 (top center), 60 (both), 65 (top left), 66 (top left), 72 (top right), 85 (top left, bottom right), 86 (both), 87 (top left), 89 (bottom right), 92-93, 95 (top left), 96-97 (left, bottom center), 103 (bottom right), 104 (top right), 105 (bottom left), 106 (bottom right), 107, 110 (center right), 112-113, 117 (top left, bottom left), 120-121, 128 (bottom), 136 (top left), 138 (both), 140 (bottom left, right), 148-149 (top left, bottom center, bottom right), 151 (bottom right), 152, 153 (bottom left), 154 (top left).
Collection of Mike Vargas: page 129 (bottom).
Alan G. Weiler: page 41 (bottom).
Courtesy Wham-O, Inc.: pages 2 (bottom left), 10 (bottom left), 12 (top left).
Eli Whitney Museum, Hamden, CT/ Photography by Robert A. Lisak: pages 2 (top right), 46-47, 56 (left), 57 (top right), 102-103 (top left, bottom center), 114-115 (top center), 137 (bottom right).
Collection of Andrew Yanchus: pages 33 (bottom right), 116 (bottom right), 118 (top left), 140 (top left, top right), 141 (top left).